Master Class

Teaching Advice for Journalism and Mass Communication Instructors

The AEJMC Elected Standing
Committee on Teaching

Edited by
Chris Roush

Published in partnership with the Association for
Education in Journalism and Mass Communication
Elected Standing Committee on Teaching
ROWMAN & LITTLEFIELD
Lanham • Boulder • New York • London

Published in partnership with the Association for Education in Journalism and Mass Communication Elected Standing Committee on Teaching

Published by Rowman & Littlefield
A wholly owned subsidary of The Rowman & Littlefield Publishing Group, Inc.
4501 Forbes Boulevard, Suite 200, Lanham, Maryland 20706
www.rowman.com

Unit A, Whitacre Mews, 26-34 Stannary Street, London SE11 4AB, United Kingdom

British Library Cataloguing in Publication Information Available

Library of Congress Cataloging-in-Publication Data Available

ISBN 978-1-5381-0052-3 (cloth : alk. paper)
ISBN 978-1-5381-0053-0 (pbk. : alk. paper)
ISBN 978-1-5381-0054-7 (electronic)

∞™ The paper used in this publication meets the minimum requirements of American National Standard for Information Sciences—Permanence of Paper for Printed Library Materials, ANSI/NISO Z39.48-1992.

Printed in the United States of America

Contents

Proceeds from Master Class *will go to fund programs for the AEJMC Elected Standing Committee on Teaching*

Introduction

Chris Roush, UNC-Chapel Hill

If you're reading this, that means that you're about to teach some form of mass communication course at a college or university and you're looking for suggestions, ideas and tips. You've come to the right place.

The Association for Education in Journalism and Mass Communication's elected standing committee on teaching has put together this textbook to improve the "standards of academic and professional preparation for teachers in the field." That statement is in the AEJMC bylaws, and until recently the committee has performed that task in a variety of ways. It has held panels and seminars at AEJMC events, and for the past 10-plus years it's also conducted a teaching contest to promote and encourage innovative teaching methods in the field.

This textbook takes those efforts a big step further. It combines—in one place for the first time—the best practices and tips for teaching journalism, advertising, public relations and other forms of mass communication. And it's written by some of the top teachers in the field, people who have won awards for their teaching at the campus, state and national level. In addition, they have interviewed their friends and colleagues across the country about teaching and culled those ideas into the following chapters.

This is a book I wish I had when I started teaching as an adjunct back in 1999 at Georgia State University and then at Washington and Lee University and the University of Richmond. As a professional journalist, I had no formal training in how to teach a writing or reporting class, and I had no idea where to go to get advice on what I need to do in the classroom or how to put together a syllabus. I had some vague ideas about how to grade, but no real understanding of how to prepare to teach each class session.

My lack of training for higher education teaching continued when I became a tenure-track professor in 2002. I was shown a sample syllabus of one of the classes I was scheduled to teach, and even given some sample exercises. But the "training" consisted of a 90-minute session with other instructors teaching the same course, and then I was given the keys to the classroom. I was scared and felt unprepared. I got better throughout the years by trial and error, by recognizing my mistakes and constantly fine-tuning my lectures and assignments.

Things have changed today at universities and colleges. Many of them now have more formalized training for their new instructors. And if you're in a doctoral program, most of those now require a pedagogy class where different teaching strategies and styles are examined.

The AEJMC teaching committee hopes that these efforts to improve the quality of mass communication instruction will be helped by this text-book. Those of us who contributed to this book love what we do. We love interacting with students, and we love seeing the quality of their work improve as the term goes on. We get a lot of psychic satisfaction out of what we do, and we hope that comes through in the pages you're about to read.

Thank you for your interest in teaching future generations of mass communicators. We can't think of a better calling.

To find teaching materials that will help you in the classroom, please visit our website at http://www.aejmc.com/home/resources/teaching-help/.

1

So, You're a College Instructor. Now What?

Karen M. Turner, Temple University

"Teaching is surprisingly difficult." That's what first-time instructors often say—be they newly minted PhDs, someone transitioning from industry or those who want to give teaching a try as an adjunct. But if you take a deep breath and keep in mind you *really do* have something to offer your students, you'll be fine. The challenge is how to effectively convey your knowledge and experience. Through the chapters of this book, we'll help you become a better teacher—and maybe even a master! Congratulations! Teaching is an admirable profession.

IT'S A CALLING, NOT A JOB

Everyone has heard the adage, "Those who can, do; those who can't, teach." This has always sounded like a criticism of those who choose the teaching profession. However, when people are asked who most influenced their life, it's usually a teacher. Oprah often talks about the impact her fourth-grade teacher Mrs. Duncan had on her life. And so it shouldn't be surprising that for many instructors, teaching is viewed as a calling.

When interviewing several journalism and mass communication instructors, the common theme was they're "in it for the students." Many of us are passionate about our charge to develop the next generation of respected, responsible, intelligent and socially aware news gatherers and communicators. We're preparing students for evolving communication professions in a multicultural global environment. Desiree Hill is a media instructor at the University of Central Oklahoma. She says teachers can have a big impact on young lives. "There are students sitting in the classroom with low self-confidence or anxiety or they may be first-generation students who don't have a roadmap of what college should be," she said. "A little bit of attention can help students blossom who might otherwise be overlooked or become frustrated and drop out."

Lydia Timmins, who teaches at the University of Delaware, says for her teaching is clearly a calling. "A job to me is a thing you do that doesn't mean anything to you. You show up, do what someone says, and go home," she said. "A calling is employment that you care about and think about and want to do well. Like journalism, teaching is a calling. Lord knows you don't do it for the money, you do it for the meaning."

But Texas Christian University journalism professor Aaron Chimbel says teaching can be both a calling and a job. "It's a calling in the sense that to do this well you have to be able to get the most out of your students, which usually requires you to connect with them in some way. You are not just providing information, you are mentor and someone they will look to for the rest of their lives," he said. "On the other hand, there are some arduous tasks that are like so many jobs, but, as I often say, the students are what make it so great and worthwhile."

Mississippi State's Deb Wenger sums up the sentiment well: "The best teachers are energized by the idea of learning themselves and excited by helping others to learn. Perhaps it is that enthusiasm that marks the differences between a 'calling' and a 'job,'" she said. "We often associate the word 'job' with something arduous and potentially unfulfilling, and though teaching can sometimes feel thankless, more often than not, teachers find themselves feeling pride in their students and end each semester with a sense of having done some important things right."

Long-time Philadelphia television reporter Walt Hunter, who retired after 45 years in the business, began adjunct teaching in 2017. He's new to teaching and says he's found his calling. "A job puts money in your wallet. A 'calling' fills your soul," he said. "The thrill of walking into that Immaculata University classroom last January, looking at those 12 faces, and realizing that maybe I could share some thought, some insight that could change their lives, still fills my heart." He adds, "Jobs come and go. But a calling stays somewhere deep inside, all your life, and, if you are very blessed and lucky, like me, someday you answer it."

University of South Carolina's Laura Smith says she always knew she would teach because teaching was in her blood. "My great grandfather was a teacher, my grandmother was a teacher, my great aunt was a teacher," said Smith. "Once he retired from the military, my father became a teacher. It's a deep and rich tradition in my family." But Smith said before she embarked on a teaching career she wanted to have substantial professional experience so her students would take her seriously.

"I felt that way about my own professors," she said. "I especially trusted the ones who had worked in the industry before entering the classroom. Those were the kind of teacher I wanted to be. So I worked in TV for about 12 years and then, when the time was right, I entered a PhD program."

A beauty of this calling is the opportunities to be innovative—we are limited only by the lack of our ability to think outside of the box! It's important to try to reach all student learners; to create a comfortable class atmosphere; to connect with students in a way that develops in them a thirst to learn, not to just get a good grade; and to foster the development of research and inquiry. Also, you will not always know the answer, and that's OK. What's important is to be a lifelong learner and model this behavior for your students.

Take chances to grow, and you'll become a better teacher.

YOU'RE NOT JUST TELLING WAR STORIES

Oftentimes, especially for those transitioning from industry, there's a tendency to tell war stories. The classroom can be a comfortable space to share our experiences with students. But as Pete Watkins, Temple University associate director in the Center for the Advancement of Teaching says, such stories must be relevant. "We remember stories better than facts," he explained. "Make sure the students make the connection as to why it was important." This sentiment was echoed by many seasoned instructors such as University of Missouri-Kansas City journalism professor Peter Morello. He spent 36 years working in the profession and 18 years in the classroom. Morello says he uses his war stories as a teaching tool. "Once students know I have been around the block, I find they are more likely to pay attention," he said.

Morello, who teaches global journalism, said sharing his experiences is a way of getting his students to understand how the coverage of local issues is effective in reporting on crises abroad. "It is often not about the conflicts themselves, but the triggers . . . such as ethnic/religious bias and division, political dysfunction, hunger and hopelessness," he said. "Over time, I have further developed more of a 'solutions-based' approach to a student's reporting skills . . . how conflicts can be resolved, how groups can learn to understand each other, steps that can be taken to avoid future conflict."

Temple University's David W. Brown maintains an active public relations practice. As such, his war stories always find their way into his teaching. "Because public relations as a profession in a city like Philadelphia is something that is always evolving, I find that my active involvement in the field allows me the opportunity to bring real-life examples into the classroom in real time—as they're happening," he said. "The war stories provide a degree of authenticity with the students that helps to provide context to the theory of the practice. For me, theory without practice provides only half of the picture."

Brown added being a practitioner and professor of color enables him to bring his unique experiences into the classroom. "That distinction adds an even more interesting twist that will help my students appreciate different perspectives in becoming more adept at navigating increasingly diverse terrain," he explained. So telling recent and not-so-recent war stories can be an effective teaching tool. The challenge is whatever stories you tell must be relevant.

FROM THE TRENCHES

Talking Shop in the Classroom

Jennifer C. Thomas, Howard University

There was a time when I was hesitant to "talk shop" outside of the newsroom. Journalists are a strange yet wonderful fraternity. We don't flinch when discussing coverage of unnerving stories. We have all worked cruel and unusual schedules and have had crazy behind-the-scenes encounters in control rooms, studios and newsrooms. We have met people in the field who give credence to the saying that "truth is stranger than fiction." We are tough, but humane. As a journalism professor, sharing "the real deal" is crucial. Discussing the stories that you've encountered in the field is a necessary part of your teaching philosophy. It helps shape the student and brings to life the stories and anecdotes in the journalism textbooks. It shows the student that you are the master of this topic, because you've "been there, done that."

I often begin my journalism courses by stating: "If your feelings get hurt easily, if you don't like getting up to report to work at 4 a.m., if you can't accept working holidays, weekends and birthdays, and if you can't accept making low salary for a high-pressured stressful job, then this may not be the career for you." I then transition to share how journalism shapes history and how we hold some of the most important roles in society.

My first year teaching was the fall of 2011. I had just earned an MA degree in journalism, after working 20 years full time as a broadcast journalist. As I was preparing the syllabus, I realized one class was taking place on the 10-year anniversary of Sept. 11. I was the 9 a.m. newscast producer at CNN on this fateful day, and hitherto had not discussed my feelings in depth. It was just too emotional. However, I decided to share and also discuss some of the ethical implications of showing graphic images then and now (the anniversary). We then shifted gears to allow each student to share a reflection of that day. To my surprise, it was one of the most impactful classes of the year. Several students were from New York City and had vivid recollections of the tragedy. We were able to discuss the media's coverage and put it into perspective. I learned valuable lessons that day—that sometimes going off-script is necessary, that students appreciate really being heard, and that experience shapes education.

Telling war stories can also be a way of sharing what not to do—your failures. Robert (Ted) Gutsche Jr. teaches at Florida International University. He said such stories "become lessons for students on how to succeed." Timmins of the University of Delaware agrees. The former news producer says her approach to sharing her war stories has changed over the years. "The students like the stories, but now I do more than just tell, I explain," she said. "I admit the wrong decisions I made, and how I tried (and sometimes failed) to correct them. I think the war stories act as a peg to hang the theory on, to show them that it's all connected."

Gutsche cautions we shouldn't overuse our war stories as a supplementary teaching tool. "If the course turns into a war story a period or the stories are dated and the stories do not focus on how students themselves can operate, improve or reflect, then the tales do nothing more than create a divide between students, the instructor and proposed innovations for the future of the profession," he said. So be mindful that war stories should be relevant, timely, to the point and short. It's not about you! Long elaborate stories can be interpreted as braggadocios.

University of Central Oklahoma's Hill said the only time she breaks the "keep-it-short rule" is when she does a breaking news module in her television production class. "I do several days on this topic, and spend one day on the Oklahoma City bombing," she said. "I was an EP at a local station during the bombing, so I share video, then do Q & A with the students after." Steve Doig of Arizona State says his war stories tend to be self-deprecating. He tells them to illustrate what students can learn from his 23 years as a newspaper reporter. "For example, in talking about the dangers of using voice recorders, I told about the time I did a high-stakes interview in a target's office and my recorder had picked up a hum from his fluorescent desk lamp that wiped out his voice," said Doig. "Luckily, I also had taken notes, which was the lesson I wanted my students to learn."

The sharing such stories doesn't have to be limited to you as the instructor. Guest speakers often bring their "real-world" current experiences to their presentations. But provide them with ground rules too. You don't want them to be long on telling war stories and short on sharing technique. If you've taught for a while, no doubt you have student war stories you can also add to your teaching toolkit. Kim Fox teaches at The American University in Cairo. She says she shares success stories with her students and provides examples of plagiarism cases. Providing student examples can be an effective way for current students to learn from the success and failures of their not-so-distant peers.

FEARS OF A NEW INSTRUCTOR

Anytime you begin a new adventure, there's some trepidation. And this is expected when you begin teaching. Even though many of the instructors and professors I spoke to are now old hats at teaching, the anxiety of being a newbie isn't easily forgotten. What if you've prepared a great lesson, anticipating a wonderful robust discussion, and the students just sit and stare? No conversation. What to do? Don't worry, it's happened to all of us. Just stay focused. You'll get through it.

TCU's Aaron Chimbel advises new teachers to play to their strengths. "Some people are great lecturers, some are great discussion leaders, some are great at breaking down examples, some are great in a lab environment," he said. "Your students will get the most out of your class if you are doing what you do best. If at all possible, don't try to teach the class how the last person did it unless that fits you or you just have to."

Smith, who teaches journalism at South Carolina, says she tells newbies that imparting knowledge takes a lot of hard work. "When we first get out of the field and into the classroom, we tend to think it's easy to learn a core skill. But it takes time and effort to teach a core concept well," she said. "You really need to sit down and think to yourself, 'how did I learn that?' 'How can I break that idea down into little, discernible bits of knowledge?' 'How can I create a hands-on assignment that helps students practice that one, small skill?'"

Arizona State's Steve Doig agrees. He said he quickly learned that "teaching isn't the leisurely semiretirement" job some of his former newsroom colleagues think it is. Michelle Bradsher-McHugh began her teaching career as an adjunct and now teaches television management full time at Drexel University. She advises as a new professor you have to "have it all together" from the beginning. You don't want to have your students start off on the first day confused or overwhelmed. She said it's important to set the right tone that first day by having everything mapped out. Bradsher-McHugh, who also teaches online, said being organized is critical when you're not having face-to-face meetings with students.

Now don't stress. Obviously, you want to be as organized as possible. But many faculty find that, depending on the course, their syllabus is a living and breathing document. (More on this later in the book.) A resource that is sometimes overlooked is the campus instructional support center. If you have one, use it. The professionals there can help make your initial teaching experience less scary.

However, as you're thinking about organizing your course, there are logistical issues you need to address. To help you get started, departments, schools and colleges usually host a new-faculty orientation event. A similar activity is often held for adjuncts, or perhaps it's held in conjunction with the new-faculty event. This is where you'll discuss and get clarification about a variety of teaching issues such as the academic calendar, code of conduct, course add and drop deadlines, mid-semester breaks, campus online and office resources, faculty policies and handbooks, classroom time requirements, canceling class, grading rubrics, awarding extra credit, midterm reports and student evaluations, exam schedules, incompletes and final grades.

Something that isn't talked about enough is what to do in case of an emergency. You should know what to do if there's an active shooter, fire or other emergency. More and more universities are proactively addressing this issue by holding simulation drills.

Another fear new professors have is balancing one's teaching with the obligation and desire to do research, especially if you're on a tenure track. Having your research inform your teaching is something new instructors hear often. But how to do this? FIU's Gutsche is well published. Over the years he says he developed a way to marry his research with his teaching. "To make it work, I matched my learning outcomes of my classes to my research objectives," he said. "If I was working on a project related to a particular set of theories or case studies, these would become central to the topics of class discussions, assigned readings, research projects of the students or reporting efforts—it engaged students in discussion and action, thoughts and debates that were well beyond themselves and that pushed their coursework and involvement in the classroom. In the end, we all won."

FROM THE TRENCHES

Overcoming the Jitters of Being a New Instructor

Soomin Seo, Temple University

I felt like a fraud. Here I was, teaching my first class as an assistant professor straight out of a doctoral program. I did attend a new-faculty orientation, but it was more about what not to do from a legal and administrative perspective, assuming we knew how to teach. It terrified me that I did not know much about the local history or culture. It scared me to think that students were paying thousands of dollars to take my class. Is it even possible to give my blue-collar students their money's worth?

Due in part to my insecurities, I created an open-ended syllabus: I told students it will be updated frequently online, reflecting the dynamic world of journalism we were studying. This turned out to be a very good thing, allowing me to calibrate the workload and difficulty of assignments as I got to know my students better. In an effort to memorize the names of my students, I made a printout of student photographs with names, carrying it around with me everywhere.

I wish someone could have told me that I should spend less time preparing class materials (i.e., reading books and articles) and more time talking to fellow professors and students to become familiar with the social fabric of my department. What did the other professors teach? What jobs do students get after graduation? Knowing these things proved crucial in boosting teaching effectiveness.

Newbie professors tend to teach dense classes with too many readings, and I was no exception. Gradually, I did learn to ease up a little, pacing my class by alternating hard materials with softer examples and narratives. I also overcame my reluctance to share personal experience, thinking I should avoid becoming the lazy journalism teacher who talks endlessly about the good old days. As it turned out, however, my students lit up when I shared my stories covering North Korea and sub-Saharan Africa as a foreign correspondent.

Still, there were days when I felt insecure or downright incompetent. On those days, I put on my best clothes and thought of the wonderful teachers I have had over the years. The professor who had more faith in me than myself, the professor who always provided two-page feedback for my essays. Some of them are no longer around, but I reminded myself that they will continue to live in me as long as I am teaching.

You don't have to be a newbie to experience the fear of staying relevant and connecting with your students. Peter Morello reminds us of the painful truth that our students stay the same as we get older.

BEING AN ADJUNCT OR INSTRUCTOR

Being a teaching assistant or getting assigned a class as the instructor of record is common when one is going through a doctoral program. Delaware's Lydia Timmins says her first experience adjunct teaching was while she was in the doctoral program at Temple. She says she thought it would be fun. "I enjoyed working with our interns at the station and figured, you know, how hard could this be?"

The challenge she found was writing the syllabus. "I was not prepared to lay out 14 weeks before the semester started," she said. "How do I know what I want to talk about three months from now? That was (and still is) the bane of my job. Then at the other end . . . grading was and is a challenge. I mean, I feel like I just 'know' when an assignment is good or not. So now I find myself loving rubrics, which I HATED when I first started teaching."

For many full-time working professionals, giving back through teaching is something they look forward to once they have the time. Denise James worked as a broadcast journalist for 30 years and always wanted to teach but knew her unpredictable schedule didn't allow for it. "For years, afternoon and evening live shots presented a constant risk that I could be late for or even miss class from time to time without enough lead time to recruit an experienced colleague to stand in for me," she said. But when her job changed she leaped at the chance to get into the classroom. She says she loves adjunct teaching because "I love seeing the proverbial light bulb go on when someone discovers or understands something new or in a new or additional way."

Mississippi State's Wenger first taught as an adjunct while still working full time as a broadcaster. Though it's been years, she said she remembers clearly when she got a call to see if she was available to take the plunge. "The biggest challenge of working as an adjunct revolved around how little preparation and guidance I was given," she said. "I literally got a call on Thursday for a class that started on Monday. The second I said yes, the person on the phone asked me what book I wanted to use! Considering I had never taught the class before, I stammered, 'Uh, can I use the same book as the last guy?' Fortunately, TV journalists are pretty good at moving quickly, so I read the book, developed a syllabus and a lecture and walked in mostly confident that Monday night."

Whatever your path to get a job as an adjunct, there are practical considerations before you set foot in your classroom.

As with new full-time professors, communication departments and schools sometimes hold a gathering to explain to adjuncts the rules and regulations, provide resource lists and answer frequently asked questions. If not, you should create your own query list that you put to the department chair or school director. Often, some of your questions may be addressed in your adjunct contract. Also, university websites and teaching centers can be helpful. You should know things such as the academic calendar, the location of your classroom, whether you need a classroom key or entry code, your student roster, course prerequisites, who checks the prerequisites, the textbooks used and how to get an instructor copy. If you're not assigned a designated adjunct office, then you need to know where you can hold meetings with students. Also, know training resources for the learning management systems used at your college or university such as Blackboard, Canvas, Sakai, Moodle, etc.

COMMON MISTAKES TO AVOID

When I communicated with journalism and mass communication professors, asking for answers to this chapter section, everyone had plenty to say! Here are samples of their pearls of wisdom:

- Don't be afraid to seek help from other instructors or institutional systems established for teacher support.
- Don't lower standards because you feel bad for a student who is trying hard but is not mastering the material. Instead, determine if there's another approach to teaching that material to the student. Or perhaps there's a campus instructional teaching center that provides help for students.
- Don't approach teaching as if you're an editor. Don't simply fix the story for students. They need to be the ones to make changes to their work. Go through it, discuss areas for improvement and why and strategies to do so, then send them back out to do it.
- Don't stress. Every semester is a chance to start over.
- Don't ignore the many rules that may seem ridiculous that have to be followed. The academy is extremely bureaucratic.
- Don't let pushy students change your mind about a grade, or how you conduct your class. Students talk and they may try you.
- Don't be afraid to admit if you've made a mistake. Apologize.
- Don't be afraid to admit ignorance. You can turn the issue into an exercise by asking the students to find the answer to discuss during the next class meeting.

- When teaching online don't assume the course will run itself once it's set up. You have to be involved with the discussion boards. You need to be engaged with online students much more than with your campus students.
- Don't drop out. Stay active in the profession. Join and work with professional organizations (Society of Professional Journalists [SPJ], Radio Television Digital News Association [RTDNA]) and affinity groups (National Association of Black Journalists [NABJ], National Association of Hispanic Journalists [NAHJ]).
- Don't ignore the changing technology. Be aware of what tools newsrooms are experimenting with and what social media and apps your students are using.
- Don't talk "at" or "down to" students. Meet them at their level.
- Don't overload the students with information. Find creative and interesting ways to convey the concepts—perhaps through an interactive class discussion rather than just lecture.
- Don't be so wedded to your planned curriculum that you miss an opportunity to "go with the flow" if the class is interested in the topic.
- Don't try to teach too much or too fast during the semester. Pace yourself. Students need repetition. They also need a *lot* of interaction.
- Make yourself available to students as much as your time allows and encourage them to meet with you, one-on-one or in small groups.
- Don't fall into the one-size-fits-all teaching approach. Recognize that students have different learning styles.
- Don't live in the university bubble and forget how artificial it can be for those in our communities. Young professors who move straight from their doctoral work to academia are usually the most susceptible.
- Don't assume because you had a successful professional career that you will be an automatic success in the classroom.
- Develop a social media policy. For example, you can Facebook friend me once you've graduated, and if you follow me on Twitter, I will follow you.
- Remember that students too have to balance their life inside and outside the classroom.
- Expose students to both the theory and practice of our curricula and college experiences. Too often the emphasis of skills due to the demands of the industry and a student's career goal undermines the personal growth and intellectual work, which is part of the university experience.
- Don't forget you were once clueless, too. Especially if you're transitioning from the profession, the challenge is to break down the "automatics" of your former job into a series of steps leading toward mastery.

- Don't take it personally. A student's perceived lack of effort is rarely about you. Many students are taking several courses and some may be navigating personal issues and distractions.
- Don't give students the answers. Let them wrestle with the concept— ask a question or give a prompt or activity.

FROM THE TRENCHES

Common Mistakes to Avoid

Kim Fox, The American University in Cairo

If you've been a part of the academy for more than five years, then you could surely make a list of "common mistakes to avoid." In my case, this short list includes some reflections from my experience along with observations from former newcomers.

1. **Preparing for class**

If at all possible, take the time to map out your entire semester in advance of the start of the semester. It's true that you should monitor your progress at about the mid-semester point and make adjustments. You want to avoid "winging" it and being just a week ahead of the students.

2. **Gossip**

It's ideal to know what's happening on campus and in your department. However, you want to avoid being a part of the gossip mill. That means trying to avoid, (especially) as a newbie, being a portal for complaints.

3. **Campus Governance**

If you are tenure track, at some point you will need to have some service to the university. One way to do that early in your academic career is to get involved in your university's faculty senate. Just being a senator and participating in meeting and committees will give you an idea of how the university functions. You want to avoid waiting until the last minute (the year before you submit for tenure) to learn the university's structure; the sooner you know how things work, the sooner you will be able to determine how to participate in campus life that is meaningful for you.

4. **Students' Rights and Professors' Rights**

It's a given that students should be treated with respect, but make sure you read up on their as well as your rights as a professor/instructor/lecturer. You want to avoid being pigeonholed and feeling like you don't have a voice on issues that impact you.

5. **Self-Care**

This is something that isn't discussed enough: how to balance course prep, teaching and other work-related responsibilities with personal interests. You want to avoid burnout by having a life outside of work/campus. You should have a network of friends who are not related to your job. You should also plan an activity just for you at least once a month, if not more often.

CONCLUSION

Teachers interviewed for this chapter had interesting things to say when I asked them what they know now that they wish they had known when they began teaching:

- "I know how absolutely fulfilling and inspiring teaching is."
  Denise James, Temple University

- "How much a part of your life the students would become. The greatest joy is following students after graduation as they begin their careers, get married, have children, etc."
  Aaron Chimbel, Texas Christian University

- "This is an amazing calling. The responsibility of turning children into adults who will go out, get jobs and change the world. Wow. I get to do that."
  Lydia Timmins, University of Delaware

- "I often leaned on advice from former professors who spent years in the industry. . . . I also found mentors who had similar backgrounds. Their advice and encouragement were vital in my first year as a full-time tenure-track faculty member.
  Jennifer C. Thomas, Howard University

- "I wish I had realized just how much teachers, at any level in a person's life but especially at the college level, really shape a person."
- "What 'Netflix and Chill' means to the current generation of college students. Seriously . . . Thank goodness for the brave young lady who approached me after class to let me know the 'trendy definition'."
  Michelle Bradsher-McHugh, Drexel University

- "I wish I knew all the individual talents of each student, and their goals and personalities, BEFORE the semester began rather than AFTER. They were, each and every one, unique, and it was a joy to discover their abilities and goals, as well as getting to know them."
Walt Hunter, Immaculata University

- "Show LOTS of student work in class, and critique it vigorously, but nicely. Teach students how to deconstruct their own work and the work of others, publicly. Today's students have pretty thin skins."
Laura Smith, University of South Carolina

- "Be very clear about 'video cheating.' For example, I've had a few students hand in a video story to me that they did for another class. I wouldn't have imagined that anyone would ever do that. Now it's stated in the syllabus, and I remind students throughout the semester."

- "When students reveal they may be suffering from depression, anxiety, or if some major stressors have occurred in their lives and they reveal those to me—I am more confident now in letting them know what options the campus offers to help them."

- "When a student asks where they stand on grading, make sure they understand it isn't guaranteed. I know that is obvious, but I always say that while they may have an A or a B now, if they don't do well on final assignments the grade will drop."
Desiree Hill, University of Central Oklahoma

- "The years have helped me to become more humble in my approach to teaching because I have learned that I am taught by the teaching process as much as I seek to teach. That cycle continues to replenish itself in new and exciting ways and, for that, I am grateful."
David W. Brown, Temple University

- "I wish someone would have told me to participate in the university/faculty senate even if only to attend a meeting every now and then. Understanding how the university works is huge . . . [t]his comes in handy for potential collaborations, teaching ideas and just meeting colleagues to hang out with for dinner and to unwind."
Kim Fox, The American University in Cairo

- "I wish I knew 10 years ago that there is a difference in our field between teaching content and socializing students to the profession. This conversation of how (and how hard) to socialize students to the profession, its expectations and its consequences is easily dismissed because the students 'are students, after all,' though we hear from industry professionals not just many students struggle to write well, but that they are slow to acclimate to a frequently rigorous and unfriendly industry mentality that does little to coddle."

- "I wish I knew earlier how to deal with [such] things [as] the extent to which grades are the determining factor for many students to indicate what they have learned. Grade inflation is a real thing—especially among faculty who are new and trying to fit in, for adjuncts trying to keep their jobs, and for those of us on the tenure track trying to curb potential classroom revolts and complaints . . . our students think the amount of time they put into their work trumps how well they did on an assignment, or that appearing in class is the same as participating."
Robert (Ted) Gutsche Jr., Florida International University

- "You need to do whatever it takes to make sure you're enjoying the students and the work. I found myself getting curmudgeonly a few years ago, grumbling about students more than I should and generally feeling disgruntled. I decided to reinvent a class I had been teaching for a while to turn it into a class I would love to take—I learned some new skills, experimented with some new approaches and generally realized that this process of reinvention needs to be ongoing."
Deb Wenger, Mississippi State University

- "[T]eaching students is different than training motivated newsroom professionals. The pros already have been self-selected into journalism and have made it over a lot of winnowing hurdles that the students have yet to face. Indeed, one of the benefits of journalism school is it gives students a chance to discover that they don't have the personality that is necessary to demand answers from a powerful person or to knock on the door of a grieving family to ask for a picture of their slain loved one."
Steve Doig, Arizona State University

You're about to embark on an exciting career, or maybe you're just looking to refresh your skills by reading this book. Yes, there will be challenges and pitfalls. But keep the wise counsel from this book in mind as you prepare for your first class or perhaps your 101st class. Keep in mind too that you are a lifelong learner. Be innovative. Take advantage of being a teacher inside and outside the classroom. Meet students where they are. Challenge and encourage your students to find their passion; to step outside their intellectual and social comfort zones; to get to know people who don't look, think and view the world as they do.

We are all Mrs. Duncan.

SUGGESTED RESOURCES

Bain, K. (2004). What the Best College Teachers Do. Cambridge, MA: Harvard University Press.

Gabriel, K. F. (2008). Teaching Unprepared Students—Strategies for Promoting Success and Retention in Higher Education. Sterling, VA: Stylus Publishing.

Hall, D. (2002). The Academic Self: An Owner's Manual. Columbus, OH: Ohio State University Press.

Pascarella, E. T., and Terenzini, P.T. (2005). How College Affects Students: A Third Decade of Research. New York: Jossey-Bass.

Weimer, M. (2013). Learner-Centered Teaching: Five Key Changes to Practice. Second Edition. New York: Jossey-Bass.

2

Preparation Is the Key

Catherine Cassara, Bowling Green State University

A famous career manual for those entering or re-entering the job market is titled "What Color Is Your Parachute"? A facetious parallel on teaching success might be titled "What Color Is the Ink in Your Grading Pen?"

The key to teaching success is preparing in more ways than one might want to have to imagine, so that when you step into the classroom you can relax and give yourself over to the performance that will capture the members of your audience and convey your message to them.

The best preparation for teaching is to identify four concepts:

1. who you are;
2. who the students are;
3. what the intended course outcomes are; and
4. how you are going to deliver your content to them.

From time to time, all four of these concepts change, so each semester they may take re-examination upfront.

You may have written a one-page teaching philosophy either as a class assignment or as part of a job application. In either case, the exercise was hypothetical, and even last semester's philosophy may be different than where you stand today. Self-reflexivity is the point of the exercise, even if you do not go so far as to write another philosophical statement before each new semester starts.

"THEORIES" OF TEACHING

When it comes to teaching, "theory" is broadly defined. Constructivists coming from educational or psychological backgrounds begin with the meeting of teaching and learning styles. The Myers Briggs Personality Test, based on the typological theory proposed by Carl Jung, offers a range of 16 distinct personality types based on how humans experience the world in the areas of sensation, intuition, feeling and thinking and can help determine your teaching style. Education theorists also think about types of learners—visual, auditory, read–write and kinesthetic. In each of these cases, some of the students may have been educated about themselves during K–12 schooling, but revisiting the topic with them in college is useful if you are trying to build community, and it only makes sense if you are going to make use of the information or help them to make use of it. Additionally, of course, there are always two sides to each equation, and the instructor's own Myers Briggs results or approach to knowledge acquisition is always in play.

Another area of educational research that any teacher should follow deals with how and to what extent students can multitask, whether while they are in class or at home studying (University of California-Los Angeles, 2006). Raised with computers and social media, students today expect that they can watch TV, work on a computer, read a book (paperback or electronic) and follow social media, and process information effectively. Researchers at UCLA found students don't learn as well when distracted.

While those "theories" have to do with the learning end of the scale, there are equally strongly held "theories" about assessment and power. In the latter case, assessment can mean EITHER student assessment OR course. There are whole books written about both, and they are worth looking up.

Grading rubrics typically take the form of a grid that identifies and describes various levels of student performance for each of a task-specific set of criteria that found their way into the university from K–12. These rubrics are a handy tool for interacting with a generation of students expecting clear explanations of how the assessment of their work is completed. One of the nice aspects of rubrics is that once you search for them online, you will be drowning in them; the universe of available rubrics will show you that there are so many ways to configure them that you will be able to find something that fits your needs. You now know that you can build rubrics that will ease your work, standardize your grading and allow you to tackle program assessment.

Program assessment is assessment of the delivery of knowledge as well as the acquisition of knowledge, BUT not assessment of the individual students. While the largest form of assessment is the institutional form that your department performs, as the first step, program/course assessment is for you. Many teachers give surveys a third or half of the way into the course to gauge students' reactions. The best of these instruments is not written negatively, but positively. So, not: "What do you dislike about this class," but rather questions like: "What else do you want to learn?" and "What could improve your experience?" or "What kinds of office hours would you find convenient—e-hours? Hours at Starbucks? Evening hours?"

Other philosophies of teaching may have a place in your classroom, depending on the topic of your course, your personality, your institution and the students in your course. Students may enter your classroom already exposed to educational philosophies that will impact their expectations of you, so these philosophies are worth knowing about.

The original challenge came from Paulo Freire in "Pedagogy of the Oppressed." Freire opposed what he called "the banking model of education" and called for a new relationship between teacher, student and society. While his work was initially focused on a call for education for the dispossessed in Latin America, his philosophy sought a problem-posing approach to education that would allow people to develop their power to critically perceive the way they exist in a world—which was not a static reality, but constantly changing.

Moving beyond Freire, bell hooks contests institutional traditions that recreate rituals of power to suppress difference. In "Teaching to Transgress," hooks challenges teachers to use education to liberate and to include instead. She is a powerful social critic, and her message conveys a spirit of hope.

THINKING ABOUT THE CLASS

The thinking that goes into the design of a course should have everything to do with who the teacher is and who the course serves—freshmen, seniors, master's or doctoral students. Any teacher might dream of a classroom where students pursue knowledge freely and independently for the sake of the exercise itself. But great teaching failures have been predicated on exactly those notions, because the teacher is only a small part of the classroom equation.

An idealistic first-time teacher could walk into the classroom and inform entry-level students: "You are free. There will be no grades. This classroom is a democracy. You are independent—go forward and learn!" In the real-world educational system, teachers must teach the class and hand out grades. So most students in this hypothetical "free" class, rather than celebrating the freedom presented to them, will worry that they are not learning what they need to know, and most will wonder how to know what their grades are. Students who typically don't worry about these issues will take advantage of the setting, doing little and expecting much—taking advantage of the lack of measures.

Some instructors approach teaching with a claim to freedom and liberation, but actually, they themselves leave the work to the students—by "assigning" topics and classes to students and groups. They themselves do not master the topics, and it is clear to students and any other observer that this is not any kind of teaching.

Teachers with expertise in this pedagogy approach it the way it is meant to be executed and commit depth, time and preparation. The challenge is that the students do the work but with company. Done well, it requires that the teacher be aware of and prepared to meet each student's interests and needs. Students are free to learn with teachers who have the time to allay fears, the knowledge to pique interest, and the skills of a master communicator to lead spontaneous discussions to bridge class skill and knowledge differences.

While we noted above that the UCLA researchers have found that social media serves as a great distraction for millennial students, they are going to use it, so teachers need to think about how to use it in a controlled fashion.

FROM THE TRENCHES

Getting Ready for the Semester

Susan Keith, Rutgers University

One of the things I do when preparing courses for a new term is to step back and think: "What do I hope students will know at the end of the course?" Then I plan backward, thinking about what assignments, revisions and feedback will help them reach that goal.

I try to think about minimal goals ("Students really must understand X or be able to do Y") and ideal goals ("Ideally, the best students would also grasp X or be able to, in addition, do Y"). This helps me be cognizant of the mix of abilities I see in almost every course. In my state university program, we have students from a mix of backgrounds. Some went to strong private high schools or high schools in wealthy suburbs. Others come from metropolitan areas with struggling school systems. So the range of understanding of something as simple as basic grammar can vary widely. As a result, I try to offer multiple ways for students to absorb the minimum requirements of the course as well as a few more challenging readings or optional assignment add-ons to challenge more advanced students.

I also do a fair amount of online-only teaching in an asynchronous environment where students choose their own times for viewing the week's lectures, taking part in asynchronous discussions and doing projects. The thing I've found most valuable in that process is preparing early. Successful online teaching in an asynchronous model depends on meticulous planning. Even students who are excited about taking an online course—because they like the topic or the schedule flexibility—can be nervous if they open the content-management system and don't see all the materials for the sweep of the course. In an ideal world, professors would spend a lot of time over winter or summer break prepping fully online courses, so that all the video lectures were recorded and readings posted before the courses started. Following that schedule allows professors to focus during the semester on student deliverables: papers, projects and other assignments.

FROM THE TRENCHES

Determining Office Hours

Lisa Hanasono, Bowling Green State University

Office hours provide opportunities for faculty and students to meet synchronously and address pertinent issues. From clarifying course concepts and preparing for exams to academic advising and mentoring, faculty and students address a wide scope of tasks during office hours. Each term, faculty can strategically schedule their office hours.

Although institutions and academic units may have specific rules and guidelines regarding the determination of office hours (e.g., at my university, we are expected to regularly hold a minimum of three office hours each week), it can be beneficial for faculty to schedule these weekly meetings in an inclusive and accessible manner. Instead of scheduling a three-block session of office hours on one day, for example, it can be helpful to spread out one's office hours over several days of the week.

I often set one of my office sessions right before or after my class meetings because students are often thinking about our class and on campus. Depending on one's student population, a faculty member may consider holding one weekly session in the evening (e.g., 5:30 p.m. to 6:30 p.m.) to accommodate students who hold day jobs or have classes during the traditional 9 a.m. to 5 p.m. time block.

Perhaps most importantly, my syllabus always indicates that I will meet students during regular office hours and by appointment. There are many apps and programs that can help faculty efficiently schedule appointments with students, such as Doodle, YouCanBook.me, and Outlook. To accommodate students who cannot travel to campus (e.g., advisees who are studying abroad, students in my online courses), offer to meet them through videoconferencing technology (e.g., Skype), over the phone or through computer-mediated channels like Web-Ex or Canvas's conferences.

FROM THE TRENCHES

Arranging Office Hours

Esen Saygin Koc, Bowling Green State University

As a graduate student and an instructor or teaching associate, I look at the issue of office hours from both perspectives.

As a student, I prefer emailing my professors and scheduling a meeting. As a teaching associate, I also prefer my students to set up appointments with me; I believe it is more convenient for both parties.

Nonetheless, some professors are extremely difficult to reach. And I have seen peers of mine look up professors' teaching schedules and then wait outside the classroom so that they can actually talk to him or her—with a guarantee of a response.

Thus, I argue that consistency between our words and actions is crucial if we are to be role models for our students. If instructors or professors do not have any scheduled office hours, they should provide their students with other ways of contacting them, such as their cellphone number, or a definite block of time in the week when their emails will be answered.

HANDING BACK PAPERS

How quickly papers are returned has a lot to do with how the long-term relationship develops between instructors and their students—this is particularly true in the case of instructors teaching journalism classes. Students put a lot of energy and anxiety into producing their work, and they want feedback. Generally, their expectations for feedback are unreasonable—and even students who turn work in late are likely to ask immediately how they did.

Students do not realize, of course, that instructors facing an assignment to grade have the same reluctance and feel the same irrational dread the students did. The good news is that research suggests that students not only don't read what we write on their papers—they also do not understand our handwriting if they try (Winter, Neal and Warner, 1996). Those findings might have been depressing in another age, but now instructors have options.

For instance, learning-management systems such as Canvas allow instructors to build rubrics portioning out points for each aspect of the assignment. For instance, did the story the student produce follow the assignment's directions? Twenty points. Did the student interview at least three sources for the story? Fifteen points. Did the student do the required Census Bureau research? Fifteen points. Is the story written following Associated Press style guidelines? Fifteen points. How are the story mechanics (grammar, spelling, punctuation, etc.)? Fifteen points. Are there any factual errors? Twenty points.

The instructor can write comments in the rubric and assign any level of points. Better yet, Canvas allows the instructor to open the student's assignment from the gradebook and there (without leaving the learning software) make comments, corrections, highlights and strikethroughs.

These comments are accessible to the students. Unlike those scrawled "awk" margin notes, students are getting explanations that are clear, coherent, fair and legible.

Millennial, or postmillennial, students require regular feedback to feel comfortable. They seem not to mind a correction if the correction is useful. They appreciate the chance to rewrite an assignment, even though most of them actually will not take advantage of that opportunity.

ETHICS AND MORALS OF FACULTY

When he taught he taught about journalism ethics. Michigan State University professor Steve Lacy would always point out that reporters needed a good foundation in ethics because they never knew when they were going to need the guidance a solid ethical framework would provide. And ethical dilemmas always arose where editors, dusty ethical manuals and time were hard to come by.

The Lacy caution can as easily be applied to teaching ethics. Knowing about the ethical concerns that weave through the endeavors of teaching and learning means instructors can ponder their teaching philosophies, design their courses, think through assignment designs and set up their grading standards with a solid understanding of what their own values are and where the pitfalls are that they are committed to avoiding.

The issues Lacy covered and the questions teachers have to worry about may be different, but teachers need to understand ethical issues connected to teaching well enough to spot them the way a good player sees a chess game unfold—several moves ahead. They will need to act when they spot the problem, because by the time it has developed—and they have a chance to consult colleagues, supervisors or teaching manuals—at least they may need to do damage control in the classroom or, worse, they may face larger problems beyond the classroom.

Ethical issues facing college instructors in journalism and communication can match those stereotypical issues any other instructors might face: (1) student-conduct minefields; (2) challenges of grading equity; (3) temptations posed around hanging out—and drinking—with students. But they also are challenged by conditions inherent in assignments, such as coaching the speech team or supervising the student newspaper.

Some issues start out as small problems visible to students but not their instructors. For instance, one new teacher trying to build classroom rapport started each class with a comment on a recent game, a sports anecdote or joke. He thought everything was going well, but women and other non-sports fans in the class became convinced early that he played favorites. When he took up going to the bar with members of the class, it was naturally a sports bar, and the die was cast. Word got to college officials that he had been drinking with underage students.

He had not carded the students, nor had the servers. So it was not clear whether it was true that the students he was with were underage or whether it had even crossed his mind that they might be. He had been carried away by bonhomie.

Bonhomie is a danger for teachers mingling with their students, particularly in bars. For while some sources define the term "bonhomie" as "outgoing" or "good-natured," others describe it as "affability to your inferiors and temporary disregard for differences of position or rank."

An episode that illustrates this is a story that filled the Chronicle of Higher Education a decade or so ago about a famous cultural scholar and her research assistant, also her doctoral student, who went to a bar with a crowd of worshipping graduate students. Drinking led to dancing, which led to an extremely intense French kiss between the professor and student—in front of a sea of witnesses. Whatever the various tellings of the story on the internet or in the media, the real story was unlikely to be told or to matter.

PICKING TEXTBOOKS AND WORKBOOKS

Graduate students and undergraduate students alike are strapped for funds to buy books. When planning your courses, be honest about how much ground you and/or your students can cover. Do not order books you will not get to, and if you assign the reading, cover it in class.

There is a glut of books for introductory classes on media in an information society, journalism in a democratic society, introduction to public relations and so forth. But the competition does nothing to lower prices. Publishers blame used-book markets for their high prices, but the participants in the market who are being pinched are the student buyers.

Text reviews suggest slick colorful books with vacuous content cost more than $200 a semester, while books with fewer color prints but more depth can be found for $70, at least for now. Interestingly, the students say they do not like the slick books, which address them the same way their high school texts did. Rather, they want to read "real" books.

It takes a bit more work to find these books, but they are out there. They just may not have been written by that professor in that communication or media program you graduated from. Make sure that if you plan to use an online text, it works for the students and that if it does not, you see that it gets fixed.

The best approach to adopting texts is to spend time on Amazon and then contact the publishers and ask them to send copies so you—or your adoption committee—can review them. There rarely seems to be any intrinsic value that makes it worth it to order a text for an entry-level course that costs more than $100, never mind more than $200.

Vision Press in Alabama has a mission to turn out paperback books that students can afford and that bring something to the field. "We do not publish routine, ordinary books by authors whose primary purpose is simply to get a book published," the publisher states on its website. It publishes books by authors who have "visions" for contributions that will add something to education—in communication law, reporting, global communication, American media history and American literary journalism history.

Whatever the cost of books, instructors should be careful to get a copy of the required text to their university's library so it can be put on reserve.

Some students cannot afford their books, temporarily or at all. One copy on reserve is not going to undercut book sales, but it will mean that one or 10 students will get a chance to study.

FROM THE TRENCHES

Treating Students as Adults

Esen Saygin Koc, Bowling Green State University

In the United States, instructors are prohibited from talking to a college student's family about the student's grades or academic progress, given that the average student is 18 years or older. This age is also the point when individuals are accepted legally as adults.

However, many times we fail to acknowledge students' adulthood and individual liberty to make choices. This spans from very general rules, such as punitive attendance policies, to more specific ones, such as mandatory rough drafts.

Ethically, as instructors we need to respect and acknowledge a student's individual liberty as an adult as much as possible by reminding ourselves that the student's freedom of choice is crucial to the individual and to the society.

PREPARING FOR THE PROBLEM STUDENTS

The young man came to my office and sat. His presence was out of the ordinary, but he said nothing particular; after 10 minutes, he left. The next day he showed up again, and the pattern was repeated. He arrived. He sat. He said nothing particular, and after 10 minutes or so—which seemed like a long time—he left.

When he arrived for a third visit, I decided the ball was in my court. I began with the same general questions I had used on the other visits—how was he? How was the semester going? But this time I gently refused to accept his vague answers.

That, it seems, was what he had been waiting for. His classes were not going well. Nothing was going well. He was trying to juggle work and school, and he and his girlfriend were having trouble. And his whole life was falling apart. He had fallen asleep at the wheel and driven his car off the road. Wrecking the car meant the police had entered the picture, and he had to go to court. He did not have any money, and every problem compounded every other problem.

Clearly, this was way beyond my capacity to handle, but I called the university counseling center, put him on the phone and made sure he explained he was calling from his advisor's office, and his advisor said this was an emergency. Without the "E" word the counseling center can make students wait for a month to six weeks just to get in to see someone who will decide what kind of help they need. (Now they get that first triage appointment in two weeks if they don't make it clear it is a real crisis.)

I also told him we would figure out how to adjust his assignment deadlines once he found his feet, but I suggested he keep in touch with me.

I learned an important lesson from this experience. Female students came to my office all the time and had no problem spilling the details of their crises before they even sat down. And while I might have thought I was the epitome of the approachable and empathetic instructor, clearly, I had blinders on that I needed to adjust. I needed to learn that for some students, silence might be an indicator of distress. In fact, time has proven there are a myriad of ways students try to communicate they are in trouble and they want help.

FROM THE TRENCHES

Sharing Your Mistakes

Brandi Barhite, Bowling Green State University

Mistakes are embarrassing, but they are also teaching moments. Students appreciate when you share information about when you messed up. This helps them learn from your mistakes and also helps them relate to you as a real person.

When I teach reporting, I always talk about the proper spellings of names. As a reporter, I would verify spelling, but I would confirm it verbally.

One time, I published a name and it was wrong. The source contacted me and yelled at me. I pointed out that I had asked her the spelling and that she had confirmed. What she told me was interesting. She said she wasn't listening. She assumed I was spelling it correctly.

From then on, I would write the name in my notebook and then have the source look at it. I learned that people "see" mistakes more than they hear them.

FROM THE TRENCHES

Communicating with Underperforming Students

Jeanette M. Dillon, Bowling Green State University

I could have called this section "failing students," but I still feel uncomfortable with claiming that action, even after teaching college students for nearly 20 years. I imagine few of us want to flunk students and that many of us spend sleepless nights trying to ward off problems for a struggling student that seem to indicate future trouble. That has been my experience, anyway, and one that I discuss here because I argue many times it is what we as teachers are reluctant to discuss—still. I have long recommended that the conversation you are avoiding is the conversation you most need to have. Thus, it is time to talk again about failing students.

I can count on one hand (and recount the names) of all of the students I have failed in all of the time I have been teaching. I have passed far more students than I have failed. However, underperforming students stand out for me because I like to converse early with them and stay on top of their progress while balancing the needs of students who seemingly have the class under control and those who make all of the assignments look easy. My point is, I do not believe any of us should focus solely on underperforming students but for me I find it easier to move goals forward for students who understand class goals and their goals than I do for students who seem to miss that goals even exist.

Grades, and the communication that accompanies them, are opportunities to converse with our students (Bain 2004; Filene 2005). Sometimes, though, students do not pay attention to accompanying communication. If I do not see a change in performance, I will ask those students to meet with me so that at least I feel comfortable that we have discussed my thoughts and addressed theirs. After written and face-to-face conversations fail, and failing grades continue, I ask for permission to bring in an academic advisor and make clear the repercussions of failing grades. I do this at the same time I fret over my responsibility for the student's progress or lack thereof.

As I write this, I think of one student whom I did not actually give an F to but rather a D, which in the student's major amounted to the same thing. The student was friendly and engaged when attending class. The student did not attend class regularly, though, and because the class was a practice-based audio production class, the student missed needed instruction that affected the quality of his audio productions. He turned in assignments that were poor by industry standards and he was not keeping up with other students in the class. As a 25-year radio veteran, I felt my failure in the student's failure yet I knew the student deserved to fail. I believed in my heart and gut I was correct in my assessment, but I did not want to turn in that grade.

When the student realized the final grade, he pushed back. At the end of the semester, the student tried to negotiate work in exchange for a different grade. I went to my teaching mentor and spent an agonizing night almost in tears as I talked and evaluated all that I had done—and the student had done—over the semester. After days of staring at the grade computations and recorded communication, I knew that the D would stand and referred the student back to my continual comments as to why.

The student was in the same class taught by me the following semester. I did not want the semester to be uncomfortable for either of us and asked for a face-to-face meeting to discuss the previous semester. The meeting could not have been better; we both agreed we wanted a different outcome. The student's class performance in the second class was much improved.

At the risk of writing what all of us know, failing is not always the end result of being honest in an assessment that assigns a failing grade to a student's performance; sometimes we need to be reminded of that so we can do the job we have been given the responsibility to do.

FROM THE TRENCHES

The Student's View

Cassie Sullivan, Bowling Green State University student

A good professor provides workable office hours or would be willing to schedule an appointment with a student outside of normal office hours as needed. During the school semesters, my schedule quickly fills up between classes, a part-time job and extracurricular activities; most office hours usually fell when I had to be elsewhere on campus or off campus to work. But if I explained the schedule conflicts, most professors were willing to meet outside of their office hours to answer my questions or advise me on papers.

Another marker of good professors includes how quickly they get back to a student who emails questions. I don't know how many times I've been working on an assignment and realized I have a question pertaining to the assignment that I need answered before the next class met or before the assignment is due. While I don't expect an answer right away, I wouldn't have to wait too long before getting a response. I've also had professors give me their personal cell phone numbers for a better way of reaching them when they didn't have to.

I was taking a class on diseases when there was a rumored disease outbreak in one of the residence halls. To get my expert source, I contacted my professor to get a background on the disease, thinking I would catch her during her office hours or be able to talk to her before our next class together. Instead, she gave me her phone number and told me to call when I needed to her help.

Anyone can stand in front of a classroom and lecture for 45 minutes, but a good professor knows how to lecture while engaging the class in different ways, by connecting the lecture to something going on in students' lives. In an American History class, my instructor likened something that happened during the early 1900s to a science fiction show that had aired for a season almost a decade ago. While I was probably the only student who got the reference and laughed, the way the instructor delivered the line was enough to make me stop before I left the classroom for the night and tell her I appreciated the joke.

A good professor also understands that life happens outside of the classroom. I was so fortunate to have a handful of professors one semester who understood that I needed to leave for a week and go back to my hometown when a friend from high school died at the beginning of the week and my step-grandmother was slowly passing away. If it were not for their approval of my absence for a week, I would not have been with my family when she passed away.

There are many things that set a good professor apart from the others. But I suppose the most impressive thing a professor can do is make me forget that the world is still turning outside of the classroom, and to make me forget to compulsively check my phone or constantly refresh my email. Only a handful have accomplished that.

FINAL THOUGHTS

The first thing you do is to go through your home and your office and throw away all the pens, pencils, and crayons in any shade of red. By tradition, teachers think they should grade in red. Family and friends always give great bundles of red markers to new teachers to welcome them to new posts.

No grading in red, for real. Read Richard Dukes and Heather Albanesi's article "Seeing Red: Quality of an Essay, Color of the Grading Pen and Student Reactions to the Grading Process" in the Social Science Journal—students read much more into red corrections than the grader ever intended. The researchers suggest the color aqua as it has no carrying power at all. Green is good, as is purple.

You can have a wonderful time in the aisle of your nearest office box store, or you can just get on your word-processing software and change the colors connected to the track changes. Better yet you can do both, since the point of preparation is to be prepared for everything.

REFERENCES

Bain, K. (2004). What the Best College Teachers Do. Cambridge, MA: Harvard University Press.

Dukes, R. L., and H. Albanesi (2013). "Seeing Red: Quality of an Essay, Color of the Grading Pen and Student Reactions to the Grading Process." Social Science Journal 50 (1): 96-100, Academic Search Complete EBSCOhost.

Filene, P. (2005). The Joy of Teaching. Chapel Hill, NC: University of North Carolina Press.

Freire, P. (1970). Pedagogy of the Oppressed. New York: Seabury Press.

hooks, bell (1994). Teaching to Transgress: Education as the Practice of Freedom. New York: Routledge.

Macedo, D. P. (2014). "Introduction." In Paulo Freire, Pedagogy of the Oppressed. 30th edition. http://site.ebrary.com.ezproxy.bgsu.edu:8080/id /10910323.

University of California-Los Angeles. (2006). "Multi-tasking Adversely Affects Brain's Learning, UCLA Psychologists Report." ScienceDaily. www.science daily.com/releases/2006/07/060726083302.htm.

Winter, J. K., J. C. Neal and K. K. Warner (1996). "Student and Instructor Use of Comments on Business Communication Papers." Business Communication Quarterly 59 (4): 56-68. Communication & Mass Media Complete, EBSCOhost.

Vision Press. "Mission." http://vision-press.com/about.

3

Writing the Syllabus

Chris Roush, UNC-Chapel Hill

Now that you've been hired to teach and you've filled out all of the paperwork with human resources, moved into your office, plugged in your computer and found where your classroom is located in the building, it's time to start thinking about the actual teaching process. Writing a syllabus will help you organize what you plan to do for the upcoming semester.

There are various ways and methods to putting together a syllabus, so in this chapter we'll cover the basics. But think of the syllabus like this: As with any form of writing, there's an art to good and bad syllabus construction. A good syllabus—especially in teaching journalism and mass communication—effectively spaces out assignments, guest speakers and other work so that none of them are bunched together at one point or another in the semester. A good syllabus should have a flow that lays out what's expected of the students in the class—and how the instructor will interact with the class. In addition, a good syllabus shows the students how the course will challenge them to think and to push themselves outside their comfort zone.

THE SYLLABUS IS A CONTRACT

The syllabus, although not a legal document, is a contract between the instructor and the students who are enrolled in the class. In accepting the syllabus from the instructor on the first day of class (and if you've stopped printing it, make sure each student knows where to find it online), the students agree to abide by the rules and regulations contained in the syllabus. Failure to abide by those rules and regulations—think deadlines for assignments and a lower grade for excessive absences—means the student faces repercussions.

In addition, the instructor also agrees to abide by the syllabus and not change the dates of when assignments are due or tests given. Many students today use a planner where they will write in the dates of major assignments and tests, and changing those, especially when you move up the dates for when those will happen, is a sure-fire way to receive lower course evaluations at the end of the semester. If you do make any changes in the syllabus after it has been distributed to the students, make sure those changes are in writing. And if you're changing the dates of assignments and tests, you should be pushing those dates back, not forward, in the calendar.

To be sure, no journalism or mass communication instructor ever strictly follows their syllabus, especially the schedule. Unexpected events such as snow days or unannounced professionals who show up on campus and want to be guest speakers happen along the way that can't be foreseen when you're putting the syllabus together. But students today don't like surprises, especially when they feel changes might be hurting their classroom performance.

Rob Wells, who teaches journalism at the University of Arkansas, says that he views his syllabus as a "firm commitment" of what he will teach each semester, but he also recognizes that the document can evolve. "Some classes can proceed faster or slower than the schedule I imagined at the beginning of the semester," he says. "I will adjust the schedule accordingly, adding or subtracting subject areas and I will update the syllabus online and inform the class about the action I am taking."

Wells, who received his PhD from the University of Maryland after more than two decades as a professional journalist, notes that he rarely adds assignments after the syllabus has been distributed. More often than not, he is cutting one or two assignments depending on the pace of the class. "This approach leaves the class more flexible to explore in more depth issues that pique the students' interest," he says.

Rachel Mersey, who teaches at the Medill School at Northwestern University, likes for her syllabus to include all of the assignments for the semester so that students can plan ahead. "I tell them that I will never increase their commitment and may, at my discretion, lessen it. They are welcome to work ahead, especially if they have personal or professional commitments that will absorb time in the future."

Here's a list of what every syllabus should include:

1. **Contact information,** such as your phone numbers and your email addresses and your office hours. It's recommended that you tell students when is an appropriate time to contact you and expect a reply.

2. **Textbooks and readings:** Make sure to delineate between required readings and recommended readings. If you're going to provide readings for the students, let them know so that they don't go hunting for them. Many journalism and mass communication classes require reading of a media outlet. If a subscription is required for online material, tell the students how to access the website.

3. **Course objectives:** These detail what the students should expect to learn during the class and the skills or concepts that he or she should be able to master by the end of the semester.

4. **Grading scale:** Students want to know how their work will be evaluated. The more specific you can be, the better. Also, let them know what percentage of his or her overall grade will come from different assignments.

5. **Attendance policy:** Detail how many unexcused absences a student will be allowed, and whether he or she will be able to make up work that they missed.

6. **Course schedule:** What's going to be covered each class period, or each class week, and when are assignments due?

7. **University policies:** This can range from your school's academic dishonesty policy to policies for students with learning disabilities. Many universities require such policies to be included on all syllabuses.

8. **Accreditation standards:** If your program is accredited by the Accrediting Council on Education in Journalism and Mass Communication, your program may require you to list the ACEJMC core values and competencies that would be covered in the class.

Let's look at some of these syllabus sections, and other important points of discussion in syllabus writing, in more depth.

ANSWERING ANY AND EVERY QUESTION

One philosophy around syllabus writing is that an instructor should include every piece of information that a student might want about the class. The reasoning is that this cuts down on any ambiguity throughout the semester should a student have a question. Of course, this also means that you've got to teach the students to go to the syllabus first when they have a question and not simply email you or send you a text!

The strategy behind such syllabus writing can also prove helpful at the end of the semester if a student is contesting his or her grade and files a grade appeal based on a policy you may have verbally told the student. If you don't have the policy in writing in your syllabus, the appeal process may end up finding for the student.

Let's say your syllabus notes that your policy is to allow for up to three unexcused absences, but it doesn't state what happens after the student has four unexcused absences. When the student inquires after class one day, you may tell the student that his or her grade will be dropped by half a letter. But if that policy is not in the syllabus, the student could appeal and win his or her case.

Length can sometimes be an issue, however, with including every piece of information about the course in a syllabus. It's common for syllabuses to run up to 10 pages. But sometimes a syllabus can be as long as 50 pages. That can be overkill, and it doesn't accomplish what you hoped for because few students will read a syllabus that long.

Make sure that the syllabus is available to the students in multiple formats. In addition to handing it out on the first day of class, make sure you post it online, either on a course website such as Blackboard or Sakai, or on your own personal website. If you have a website for the course, post it there as well. This will cut down on questions throughout the semester if the students know how to access the syllabus.

FROM THE TRENCHES

A Balance between Structure and Creativity

Tracy Lucht, Iowa State University

In general, I try to strike a balance between being clear and specific in my syllabus while giving myself the flexibility to make course corrections as needed. Here are some additional thoughts:

For me, course planning requires a balance between structure and creativity. The best teaching, in my view, is inspired by the students sitting in the classroom and by events happening outside the classroom. That requires a certain responsiveness on my part throughout the semester. At the same time, I know students will not be able to focus on the content of the course if they are unsure of my expectations or always wondering what's coming next.

For example, I like to enforce deadlines (I generally do not accept late work), so I schedule assignments at the beginning of the semester and make the due dates clear. The clearer I am at the outset, the easier it is for me to uphold my standards. Yet I also give myself permission to change the nature or parameters of an assignment to serve the needs of a particular group of students at that point in the semester.

Attendance policies are perhaps the part of the syllabus that students will ask the most questions about during the semester, so make this as clear as possible. And there are many different ways to enforce attendance. Some instructors like to use sign-in sheets that require students to provide their signature next to their name each class period. Others will use electronic devices, particularly in large lecture classes, that ask students to answer questions as a way of checking attendance. And then there are those instructors who don't believe in taking attendance at all and feel that students should act as grownups and be responsible for the material whether they're in the class or not. You decide what works best for you.

Lois Boynton, who teaches public relations and ethics at the University of North Carolina at Chapel Hill, uses the following language in her syllabus:

You may be absent from class *three times* ("excused" or "unexcused") before I take points off for missed classes. **Please note**, however, that you are still held accountable for any material covered during classes, and you will lose credit for any in-class assignment or other activity completed during classes you do not attend. It is your responsibility to sign in each class period. You do not have to notify me of your reasons for your absences, nor do you have to provide a doctor's note. Use your absences wisely. If you know you need to be absent for university-related activities or other obligations, be sure to factor those into your absences. For each class you miss after three, your final grade will be lowered by three points. For example, if your grade average is a B- (81) and you have four absences, your final grade will be altered to a C+ (78).

Please note: Chances are EXCELLENT that you will need all of your absences for sick days or other types of emergencies or opportunities. I strongly suggest that you save your absences for these purposes. DO NOT waste your absences on "the weather's too nice (or too lousy) to come to class" and then ask for an exception to the attendance policy when you actually come down with the flu.

What's good about Boynton's attendance policy is that it's clear but also shows some of her teaching philosophy and her personality. She recognizes that students will want to miss class for one reason or another, and she asks them to be cognizant of their responsibilities by taking her course. She also uses ALL CAPS to emphasize her point, but she doesn't overuse them because she doesn't want to come across as if she's shouting at the students.

Carol Pardun, who teaches advertising at the University of South Carolina, likes to use in-class assignments as a way to measure attendance. She tells her students that they will have at least 12 opportunities to take an unannounced in-class assignment. She also tells them that she will only grade the top 10, which means they can miss twice without penalty. There is enough flexibility that this approach easily covers "excused" as well as "unexcused" absences.

The assignment is always easy and informative, added Pardun, and usually takes only about 10 minutes to do. "I always give it at the end of class, never giving any warning whether I am planning to give one," she said. "I grade them at three levels (better than expected, what's expected, lower than expected) and I don't write any comments on it so the grading goes fast. I average them together at the end and the student gets an A, B, or C (or lower if fewer than 10 assignments are turned in). I also make sure to give these without a pattern (not every second day for example). Students like this approach and have typically responded positively once they know they don't need to study for the assignment."

Another must-include in the syllabus, as Iowa State University professor Tracy Lucht noted, is your policy for accepting late work. Some instructors will allow students to make up work—within a certain time period, such as one week—if they miss a class as long as they let the instructor know beforehand or by the time the class ends why they're not there. Others will deduct a certain number of points from an assignment for every 24-hour period that the work is late while others will not accept late work at all, noting that journalism, advertising and public relations work in the professional world is all done on deadline and the students must meet those times. Again, this is a personal preference for the instructor to decide, but it's good to check with your program to see if it has a universal policy on late work.

Here is what Joel Geske, who teaches advertising at Iowa State, puts in his syllabus:

> Late projects are not accepted and will receive a "0" score. You don't tell a client you didn't have time to work on his or her account! If you are ill or die, please inform me before the due dates. WORK AHEAD . . . you do not produce your best work in the last five minutes!

Lastly, if your course is heavy with writing assignments, make sure that your syllabus sets parameters—what the students can and can't do—for those. Answer the following questions in the syllabus: Can they email you or call you with questions? Can they have another student look at their work and provide feedback? What types of sources are they supposed to use? When the assignment is due, can they email the work to you? Should they post their work on the course site?

COURSE OBJECTIVES

Course objectives should be listed on the first page of the syllabus, typically right after the instructor's contact information. The course objective lets the enrolled students know what the course is going to cover, and it also sets parameters for what the instructor should be teaching.

Wells from the University of Arkansas likes to include specific "learning objectives" as his course objectives in his syllabuses. Here's what he uses for his "Data Journalism" course:

- *Proficiency with relational databases*
- *You will build new databases from disparate sources such as U.S. Census and federal regulatory files. You will learn best practices for database creation and management*
- *Data gathering and extraction*
- *You will learn how to obtain and process difficult datasets, such as scanned PDF documents or non-structured text files, and process them into databases, spreadsheets and data visualization files. You will also learn basic web scraping techniques.*
- *Geocoding and mapping*
- *You will learn how to geocode data and produce interactive maps suitable for web publication via the Tableau Public platform*
- *Coding*
- *You will be introduced to the basics of computer coding via the Python programming language. Python will be used to execute basic data gathering and web scraping scripts.*
- *Data story telling*
- *You will have the basic skills to learn the benefits and pitfalls of using data to report stories. You will learn basic numeracy and how to avoid common problems with numbers. You will learn best practices for fact checking data.*

Robert McKeever, who teaches graduate and undergraduate courses in quantitative research methods, media and society, mass communication theory, and health communication at the University of South Carolina, noted that he learned about Bloom's Taxonomy of Educational Objectives when he was a doctoral student. When he started teaching at South

Carolina, he learned even more about writing objectives this way from the university's Center for Teaching Excellence (CTE).

"I try to use this method whenever I develop a new syllabus," said McKeever. "It is based on the idea that written course objectives or learning outcomes should consist of a subject (the student), a verb that is related to a cognitive process involved in learning, and an object (i.e., course content or knowledge students should have by the end of the course). The cognitive processes involved in learning, listed in order of complexity, are as follows: Remember, Understand, Apply, Analyze, Evaluate, Create."

As a result, McKeever tries to make sure his course objectives or learning outcomes section of his syllabuses use verbs that represent these processes, and that he is covering all or most of these processes in each course. "Of course, the level of depth and mastery of course concepts may vary based on course topic, level, class size, and so on," said McKeever. "But even large or introductory courses can help students achieve at least a few of the cognitive processes mentioned above to help them understand course content well by the end of the semester."

When writing course objectives, it's often easier to write them for a task-driven skills class than for a critical thought–driven conceptual class. But each course, whether it's a skills course or a conceptual course, should have four or five course objectives or learning outcomes. For example, a media ethics course would include objectives such as being able to "integrate ethical foundations and apply those ideas to professional situations" and "critically analyze current media professional practices through reading and discussing communication topics found in trade journals and other media." But a public relations writing course would include course objectives such as being able to "quickly produce any of the professional written materials required in the public relations profession" or "integrate strategy into communication pieces to target appropriate/diverse audiences and media and to effectively advocate a cause."

STATING YOUR TEACHING PHILOSOPHY

The course objectives or learning outcomes are sometimes followed by the instructor's teaching philosophy—either for the specific course or in general. And it's good to let the students know about your teaching style. Will this be a class where you lecture all the time? Or do you want the class time to be more of a conversation with the students where you get them involved in the discussion by asking them questions? The subject matter can sometimes determine what the best teaching strategy is for a course, and it may not be how you've taught classes in the past.

Your teaching philosophy or strategy will factor other parts of the syllabus as well, so think about how you plan to teach when writing the syllabus. An introductory newswriting class often requires students to write during class periods, which means that the instructor must act more like an editor, peering over the students' shoulders to look at their writing and providing feedback. But a class on media literacy likely has less in-class work and may require the instructor to call on students at several times during a lecture or session to get a discussion going.

If you've not yet written a teaching philosophy statement, now may be a good time to do so. Many universities require a teaching philosophy statement as part of an instructor's curriculum vitae. It doesn't have to be long—a page or two is the norm. But it should focus on what you as an instructor hope to accomplish in the classroom. How do you plan to get students to start thinking more critically when they're reviewing a media message? What will you teach them about finding information, or working with a client? In his teaching philosophy statement, Wells from Arkansas writes, "Part of the joy of teaching involves figuring the way to connect with students and inspire them to embark on their own original research. I use every means at my disposal, from chalkboards to video clips, discussion groups to individual presentations, to get students to internalize the material."

Lucht at Iowa State uses a "course philosophy" statement in her "History of American Journalism" class that explains a lot of her teaching style. The class is a hybrid, or blended course, so it meets online and in face-to-face class sessions. She states, "You will not just *learn* history; you will *make* history—through our own interpretations of primary sources, your own history research, and your completion of multiple assignments that will give you a chance to apply what you are learning." From this statement, the students understand that Lucht wants them to understand the importance of history while doing research on different topics. Later on in the syllabus, she tells students that she's not interested in them memorizing facts. It's "more important that you understand overarching themes, narratives and arguments."

Mersey at Northwestern makes it clear that her teaching philosophy is interactive in the syllabus for her "Philosophy of Modern Journalism" class when she asks students to tweet about what they're reading and what they're thinking. "Pay attention to the audience you attract and the feedback you receive," says Mersey in her syllabus. Although some instructors discourage use of technology in the classroom, Mersey asks her students to have either a phone, tablet or laptop with them in class so that they can interact with each other online.

Using technology to teach, though, can be frowned upon by other instructors. One instructor at UNC-Chapel Hill tells his students in his syllabus that if their phones audibly ring in class, he gets to answer and talk to the person who is calling. Other instructors ban technology such as laptops during class time, feeling that they distract the students, while other instructors allow laptops and tablets to be used for notetaking and to look up facts. Again, you decide on what will work best for you in your course and incorporate it into your teaching philosophy section of the syllabus.

READING MATERIALS AND THE COURSE SCHEDULE

Every syllabus should include a reading material section detailing the textbooks, articles, books or websites that the course will use as well as any supplemental items. You'll have to determine the textbooks and books months in advance of teaching so that the campus bookstore can get them stocked for students to purchase. Or if you plan to put together a packet of reading material, obtaining the reprint permissions and getting them all copied and bound is also an arduous task. Gung-ho students may want to know what they should be reading as soon as the previous semester ends so that they can get a jump on the work.

Picking a textbook can be a simple process if there's just one or two in the field covered by the class. But in other journalism and mass communication areas, such as introductory newswriting or public relations case studies, there are multiple books competing for space on your campus bookstore shelf. You can contract publishers and ask for a desk, or review, copy of the textbooks that interest you if you've never taught the subject before.

Textbooks aren't a requirement. If you feel as if none of the current offerings adequately cover the material you want to teach in your course, feel free to put together your own list of required readings from books, magazine articles, industry publications and websites. There's been many a college instructor who so disliked the available textbooks that they ended up writing their own and advancing the field's education.

Spell out all reading and multimedia materials into two categories: required and optional/recommended. For any required text or multimedia materials, include the estimated price in the syllabus to let students know you are aware of the expense. Geske, who teaches advertising at Iowa State, notes on his "Advertising Creativity" syllabus that students will be required to do considerable color printing, which can be costly, for their final project.

Increasingly, many journalism and mass communication classes are taught using specific software, such as Final Cut Pro for broadcast courses or software that allows students to build websites. If your students need to purchase that software, let them know in the syllabus.

One final note about reading material: In your course schedule, make it clear by what class meeting date you expect specific readings to have been completed. If the students have done the reading, that will facilitate the discussion that day.

Course schedules are a must in the syllabus. They don't need to be detailed, but students will want to know what chapters of the textbook that they should read for each week of class and when assignments will be due and exams will be taken. Some instructors will plan their course schedule on a weekly basis, while others include a course schedule in their syllabus that details what will be covered in every single class meeting. Do what works best for you.

Laura Ruel, who teaches multimedia courses at UNC-Chapel Hill, has developed a course schedule for her "Video/Graphic Information Gathering" course that is 14 pages long. Each day on the syllabus includes videos to watch and homework assignments that can be accessed via links in the syllabus. Assignments are marked in bold with the word "ASSIGN" and include the date when they are due. The schedule is so thorough that there is no ambiguity about what is expected of the students.

Remember that your schedule can change. Just because you've put it in writing in the syllabus doesn't mean you have to strictly adhere to it throughout the semester. It's smart to put a note at the end of the schedule explaining that the timetable is subject to change due to unforeseen events or the need to spend less/more time on a particular subject than what you originally estimated.

GRADING SCALES AND RUBRICS

In today's society, students seem more focused on their grades than actual learning. And grade inflation—the overall rising of average grades received by college students in the past three decades—remains a real issue. So setting up your grading scale for individual assignments as well as how a student's overall grade will be determined in a course is valuable material needed in any syllabus.

Let's start with grading scales.

A grading scale sets out for students what constitutes A work, B work and so on. The more specific you can be with your grading scale, the better. You'll want to communicate the difference between grades as clearly as possible. For example, an A grade may be cleanly written or structured and have no misspelled words, punctuation errors or AP Style errors, while a B grade may have several of these, but a C grade may have multiple such errors. An F paper may be distinguished by a fact error—a misspelled name or an incorrect age or score. In addition to letter grades, many universities and mass communication programs also use numerical scales. Check with yours to see if they have a universal numerical grading system. Some programs also delineate when to use plusses and minuses for grades. A B+ may be a grade between an 88 and a 90, while an A- is a 90 to a 92.

Here's how one journalism class syllabus breaks out its grading scale:

A = Story could be published in a major metropolitan newspaper or magazine;

B = Minor editing needed, but is publishable. Conclusions may be weak;

C = Needs extensive editing and rethinking. Structure or conclusions may be flawed. May contain spelling error;

D = Story needs to be rewritten and re-reported all the way through. May contain more than one spelling error;

F = Story has a fact error, or misstates facts from documents. Seriously flawed in writing and conclusions.

If you're teaching a class that has multiple sections being offered that semester, then the syllabuses may be using a uniform grading scale. For example, many writing courses with multiple sections use a grading scale that counts off the same number of points—2 points for an AP Style error or 5 points for a misspelled word—or adds the same number of points—5 points for a nice lead—for each class.

You'll also need to let the students know in the syllabus how their final grade will be determined. This involves breaking out what percent of the final grade will come from each assignment, quiz, event or test, and whether student participation counts for anything. Many instructors use student participation as a way to note attendance—attending 27 out of 30 class periods means the student will earn 90 percent in student participation.

Here's how Ruel, who teaches the "Video/Graphic Information Gathering" course at UNC-Chapel Hill, breaks out student grades in that class:

- **Participation, in-class exercises, homework:** 10% of final grade
- **Video Scavenger Hunt:** 10% of final grade
- **Video interview footage:** 10% of final grade
- **Video edited story (interview with supporting b-roll footage):** 20% of final grade
- **Web project #1:** 10% of final grade
- **Web project #2:** 10% of final grade

- **Graphic project:** 15% of final grade
- **Final project:** 15% of final grade

While this breakout is typically more than what you'd see in other journalism and mass communication courses, it does allow the students to do poorly on one assignment and still receive an A or B overall because there's no one part of the course that is more than 20 percent of the overall final grade. Classes where the overall grade comes from 50 percent or more of a final project or an exam may put too much weight on that part of the course.

Avoid making class participation more than 10 percent or 15 percent of the course. If it's a larger percent, then some students may try to monopolize the course discussion as a way to ensure that they receive the maximum number of points.

Many instructors these days use rubrics that provide students feedback on their grades and why they received a specific score. Rubrics can be helpful in eliminating any subjectivity in grading, particularly if you give the rubric to the student before the assignment is due so that they know what to expect. If you've not put together a rubric before, ask a fellow instructor to see one of theirs. They can also speed up the grading process.

Note how Mersey's rubric includes four different categories where students can earn points, and it also provides a range of work performance. By including this in the syllabus, or at the end of the syllabus, she's set the bar for her students of what is acceptable work, and what is not.

Here's one last thought about grading: Many mass communication classes, particularly in advertising and public relations, use a peer evaluation approach to assess student work, usually their final projects presented at the end of the class. If you plan on using peer evaluation for any assignments during the semester, make that clear to the students in the syllabus. And make sure that students can't vote for their own work. Typically, more than half of all of the students will receive at least one vote, and the best work stands out from the others.

CLASS PARTICIPATION RULES

Let's discuss participation some more, as it is often one of those nebulous parts of running a class that should be defined more clearly in a syllabus.

Class participation can mean a number of different things, depending on the class, its structure and the assignments. So the more guidance you can give on the syllabus about what's expected, the better. For some instructors, class participation is simply how much a student talks in class as part of its discussion or how often he or she answers questions. If some

Directions from the syllabus: "This assignment is designed to help you apply the concepts from the lectures, discussion sections and readings on the sources of news today and how they serve their audiences. It will also hone your perceptual skills allowing you to notice more in the media landscape.

Go to a newsstand and find a news product. This should be a print product but beyond that, it may be whatever you want: a newspaper, magazine or pamphlet on any topic and for any audience. Use all of your senses to collect data about the product. Pay particular attention to what you see and what you read, but don't neglect details such as the feel or tooth of the paper. Use evidence from this exploration to explain what audience you think this news product serves. Your analysis must apply a range of concepts from the class.

Only once you have completed your hands-on examination, research the parent company, or owner, of the news product you studied. Does knowing the parent company change your perception of the potential effectiveness of the news product to serve its audience? To answer this question fully you may need to dig into other things the parent company owns.

Carefully write up your evaluation in no more than two typed pages. Your assignment should be in 12-point Times New Roman font with 1-inch margins, double-spaced. Terms from the class and the readings should be used in your analysis and put in **bold** font in order to reinforce your use of the material. Do not just drop in terms. Be sure to explain how that concept leads to your conclusions. You do not need to turn in the print product with your assignment but you should specifically reference its title and date in your evaluation. Bring a hard copy to hand in at the beginning of your discussion-section meeting on Wednesday, Oct. 28. Assignments will be graded based on completeness, content, use of class material and grammar."

	Superior	Good	Fair	Needs work	Total
Content and ideas from the readings and lecture (up to 10 points)	Explanation and analysis incorporates key concepts from class readings & ideas from class discussions and demonstrates a clear understanding of what the concepts	Uses concepts from class but does not demonstrate clear understanding of what concepts mean.	Uses few concepts from class and does not demonstrate an understanding of the concepts.	Rarely uses concepts from class.	
	10-9 points	8.5-7.5 points	7-6.5 points	6 and fewer points	
Use of evidence for argument (up to 10 points)	Uses detailed, systematic evidence from the news product to explain and illustrate argument.	Uses some details and evidence from the news product to explain and illustrate argument.	Uses little evidence as part of the argument or uses evidence inappropriately	Does not use evidence.	
	10-9 points	8.5-7.5 points	7-6.5 points	6 and fewer points	
Style and structure (up to 5 points)	Ideas conveyed logically and points argued clearly. Well written with few spelling or grammar errors.	Argues points but lacks some clarity or is repetitive. Some grammar/spelling errors.	Difficulty in arguing points clearly and logic not apparent. Many grammar/spelling errors.	Paper is unreadable.	
	5 points	4.5 points	4-3 points	2 and fewer points	
Completeness (5 points)	Fully completed the assignment and class terms in bold; followed instructions. Turned in on time.	Completed most of the assignment. Turned in on time.	Part of assignment incomplete; did not follow some instructions. Turned in on time.	Incomplete or turned in late.	
	5 points	4.5 points	4-3 points	2 and fewer points	
					/30

Sample rubric from Rachel Mersey at Northwestern University

students aren't offering to answer questions or provide opinions, make sure you call on them.

But class participation may also involve discussions, team problem-solving sessions and short oral reports. It may also include brief blog posts or quizzes. Class participation could also involve a student giving a short update on the day's news for each class. Make sure that you've clearly delineated what counts for class participation and what doesn't.

Northwestern's Mersey relies on a number of in-person techniques but also uses software called PollEverywhere. In a large classroom, it's a means for students to engage throughout the lecture with direct results in the slide deck. On the first day of one of her classes, for example, the students must reply to a PollEverywhere question that asks, "How much do you want to be a journalist?"

Pardun at South Carolina grades student participation on a combination of attendance and Twitter activity in her advertising account-planning class. The class has a hashtag that the students use. Their participation depends on how often they tweet, how clever their tweet is, how connected the tweet is to the topic of the class and how often the tweet is retweeted or liked. "I encourage them to live tweet in class if they want, and I am constantly surprised at how good they are in discerning the key issues of class," said Pardun. "They also comment on each other's tweets. It's encouraging to see them engaging with the material and their fellow students via Twitter."

Pardun believes this class participation strategy is effective because the students also learn more about analytics than they knew before the class. "I used to assume that college students were digital gurus, but I have since discovered that they need to learn quite a bit about how to use the digital space," she said. "They end up learning all sorts of things they didn't expect to—and they end up participating a lot more in class as well. I make sure to periodically show the Twitter feed via Power Point to remind them what makes a good tweet."

Boynton provides her media ethics students at UNC-Chapel Hill a guideline of her participation expectations, and she evaluates both in-class and online participation, which can be a good strategy, particularly for those students who do not like to speak up in class. For example, the A students participate in most of the class discussions during nearly every class period (or try to participate by raising their hands often when questions are asked) and/or contribute on Sakai Forums at least twice weekly. Consistency is the key. "They contribute interesting and/or thought-provoking ideas and occasionally bring in outside material relevant to the class and to the readings," said Boynton. "They don't talk simply to hear their own voices, and they do not take over the discussion, but let others have a turn."

B students, said Boynton, participate in some of the class discussions each week and/or contribute on Sakai Forums at least once or twice weekly, but either are not at quite the same level and/or comments are not always as insightful as the A students. However, they still have some interesting things to say or questions to ask whether in class or online.

Boynton also asks her students to submit a participation self-assessment at the end of the semester. This self-assessment is completely voluntary, and about two-thirds of the students will provide their input. "I've been happy to see that those who provide their assessments do not inflate their scores," said Boynton.

PLAGIARISM AND CHEATING

A section on your plagiarism and cheating policy is a must for any syllabus if you want to maintain academic integrity. While this can often be covered by including your university's honor code or policy on plagiarism and cheating, it's often not enough, particularly in today's world where students can easily find content online. And failure to include a plagiarism and cheating policy in the syllabus makes it much tougher to enforce if an incident arises.

McKeever of South Carolina had simply included a paragraph about academic honesty and integrity in his syllabus, and typically quoted the university honor code directly, for several years. However, one semester he had a few instances of students plagiarizing from online sources. "After speaking with these students, I realized more emphasis on plagiarizing (particularly from online sources) was needed," said McKeever. "I now include a sentence about plagiarizing in bold in this section of my syllabus, and I try to make sure I go over this part of the syllabus verbally early in the semester as well."

McKeever's syllabus includes the following statement, "Please remember that plagiarism is a form of academic dishonesty and includes, but is not limited to, paraphrasing or direct quotation of another's published or unpublished work without full and clear acknowledgement."

What many syllabuses fail to include in this are the repercussions for plagiarizing or cheating. Make sure your policies are aligned with those of your program or university. Some will say that the student receives a failing grade on the assignment on the first offense and fails the class on the second offense. Others have a policy that states that the student fails the class and is reported to the university's honor court.

Because we teach in a field where content is valuable, a "zero tolerance" policy on plagiarism and cheating is advisable. That means the first time a student is caught plagiarizing words or cheating on an assignment, they should be kicked out of the class and given a failing grade.

Some programs go beyond plagiarism and cheating in their syllabuses. The Medill School at Northwestern, for example, has an academic and integrity code that all students must follow. Temple University's journalism department has issued a code of ethics to each student. At the University of Maryland, all students are asked to sign an academic integrity pledge at the beginning of the semester that will cover all assignments in a course.

FINAL THOUGHTS

Just because you've finished your syllabus and printed copies for the students doesn't mean your work here is done. The best instructors are constantly changing and tweaking the syllabuses every semester based on their experience in the classroom and the course evaluation feedback that they've received. If your university offers a faculty center that will review a syllabus, take it there and ask for constructive criticism as well.

Maybe one assignment didn't work out as well as you planned. Or maybe you realized too late that you put too many assignments in the first half of the semester and not as many in the second half of the semester when the students started to get into the subject but didn't have as many opportunities to show what they had learned. Don't hesitate to critically assess what worked and what didn't the previous semester, and don't hesitate to tear up a syllabus and start over.

With the rapidly changing world of journalism and mass communication, you're doing your students a disservice by continuing to teach the same assignments from the same syllabus over and over again.

ONLINE RESOURCES

A number of journalism and mass communication programs place their syllabuses online in a central repository for students. But this can also be a good way for instructors to look at syllabuses of courses similar to what they're teaching and glean new ideas.

Here are some places to go:

Florida: http://www.jou.ufl.edu/academics/course-syllabi/
North Carolina: http://parklibrary.mj.unc.edu/course-resources/syllabi/
Temple: https://smc.temple.edu/journalism/syllabi/
Texas: http://journalism.utexas.edu/undergraduate/undergraduate-course-syllabi

4

It's Your Classroom: Have Fun

Charles N. Davis, University of Georgia, and
Earnest L. Perry, University of Missouri

It's your first day of class—and the nerves are palpable. You're visibly shaking as your eyes track across a sea of young, dispassionate faces, all seemingly longing to be somewhere else at precisely this moment.

We've all been there. We still battle nerves, every semester, as we approach the first day of class, and we've been teaching for decades. First, simply accept the fact that a classroom can be intimidating, and use that to your advantage. Turn it into a strength. Come out with as much energy and enthusiasm as you can muster, weave in some humor if that's your thing, but for God's sake, if you do nothing else, bring your A Game on Day One.

Why? Because you simply must own your classroom. You begin creating an environment for learning from the moment you step through the door, and do so every moment thereafter. It can be a magical place where students learn from you and from one another and where you serve less as a "sage on a stage" and more as a helpful and nurturing mentor—but only if you make it so.

Intentionality is the key. Some effective teachers script entire class sessions; others, ourselves included, work from a set of class objectives for each session. It's not important which option you choose, but it's vitally important that you choose. It's the first step in learning to become intentional and strategic in everything you do in a classroom. Once you embrace intentionality, you'll find in time that you no longer have to think through all of this—it simply becomes how you teach.

How intentional? Here is a first day of class checklist. At least a couple of days before class begins, we are always going to:

- make sure I know the building and visit the classroom, obtain a key and test drive the technology.
- obtain a cell phone number for the person in charge of the technology.
- find the restrooms.
- check textbook orders in bookstore.
- ensure that the class site is completely up-to-date and that all links are still live.
- check the sound and carry of my voice in the classroom and make a call as to whether I am going to need a microphone.
- get a class roster and start learning names.
- print out anything I am going to hand out on the first day and have ready to go.

This level of preparation calms an instructor and gets them ready for the first day of class so that they can then focus on content rather than logistics.

THE FIRST DAY OF CLASS

More simple mistakes are made in the first 15 minutes of classes than at any other time, and often they are made with the best of intentions. The new instructor often is advised to "take charge," to "set expectations" or to "manage the classroom" as if the goal were to play defense against a bunch of disinterested millennials.

They may well seem disinterested, but really they are feeling you out, frankly expecting the minimum sort of effort ("Here is the syllabus. See you next class . . .") and waiting to see if you are different in any way. So be different, right out of the gate.

Here is an example: Every teaching guide you read encourages the new instructor to arrive at class early, as much as 15 minutes early, to signal eagerness and have time to write your name on the whiteboard beforehand. Students expect that—so we do the opposite. We stride in the minute class begins and talk to the class even as we are entering. It's a bit disorienting, and that's often the goal. Our style could best be described as "keep them slightly off kilter at all times." Yours may be entirely different—and again, that's OK. The key is to take time to understand your style, then embrace it fully.

Another example: Rather than start prattling on about the syllabus, begin with some exercises designed to get to know the students. Ask them where they are from, what they intend to study and most importantly, get them talking to one another and to you. It's all about building the culture of your classroom, in the end, and creating a rapport. So spend the first few minutes just getting to know your students. We had a colleague once who took pictures of every student in the class, then made flash cards and took a name quiz every class until he scored a perfect grade. That is a brilliant, disarming way to begin a semester.

Make sure to take a few moments to tell the class about yourself. Walk them through the steps that led you to the classroom, and share some information about your life—not your degrees and all the places you have worked, but your life: your family, your pets, your hobbies, what you're reading, and what's exciting you as you begin teaching. An introvert? That's OK. Share just a little, but you've simply got to lower your guard a bit and let your students know something about you. The days of the imperious, arrogant showoff (if ever there were those days!) are long since passed.

Around the 30-minute mark, it's time to transition to the course, its requirements, the text and all of the requisite material. But again, rather than simply laundry list, take another opportunity to engage the students in a bit of a game by asking for volunteers to answer a series of questions about the syllabus designed to get them digging into it and extracting the key points:

- What are the required assignments, and what is each worth?
- What are the texts? When do I read which?
- What are the major deadlines?
- How am I graded?

Once you've hashed out the syllabus, then ask whether you missed anything. Do this often, every class session. It's always surprising how many things need further explanation, and it sets the right tone.

Speaking of setting the tone on the first day, don't dare leave for the day now! If you have even a few moments left, use them engaging the students. We prefer a Socratic dialogue of sorts, in which we introduce one of the course's first elements and then asking students what they know about it. If no one jumps up to engage, then call on someone, now. Don't hesitate to call students by name, and ask for some response. It lets them know that participation will not be voluntary, but a mandatory expectation. Once you break the ice that way, you'll find it easier each time.

Finally, conclude the first class by sharing your contact information and office hours. Stress your availability and willingness to talk. Underscore the fact that you want them to come by, to email and to shoot you interesting links related to class.

Always, always end class by thanking the students for their attention and participation. Encourage the behaviors you desire by rewarding them, and especially on the first day of class.

A final tip on the first day: don't be in a hurry to get anywhere afterward. Hang out and see who comes up to chat. We've had some incredibly meaningful interactions immediately following first-class days with students we've known for decades now. Some were scared to death and wanted reassurance. Some were wanting to talk to me about a learning disability issue or a conflict down the road. All get our undivided, unhurried attention, and again, that sets the tone. It also gains valuable student touchstones, as we find that we can lean on those students in the next class session when we need someone to speak up.

Now, that wasn't so bad, was it? You've created an active, involved classroom, signaled your empathy and personality, and hopefully left them thinking this class is going to be different from any other they have taken.

BE PERSONABLE AND AUTHENTIC

Day Two is, in many ways, more important than Day One, for you are now given an entire session to signal to your class what's coming. We're a huge fan of fairly well scripting the first few minutes of that first "real" class session, inspired by the wonderful essay "Small Changes in Teaching: The First 5 Minutes of Class." I am reminded of the essayist, James M. Lang, and his emphasis on the first five minutes of class:

> It seems clear, then, that we should start class with a deliberate effort to bring students' focus to the subject at hand. Unfortunately, based on my many observations of faculty members in action, the first five minutes of a college class often get frittered away with logistical tasks (taking attendance or setting up our technology), gathering our thoughts as we discuss homework or upcoming tests, or writing on the board.

Logistics can wait. Announcements and administration can wait. Instead, leap into the subject matter, ideally with a gripping anecdotal example or a gripping story or with a puzzling question. Grab them, bring the energy level up as high as you can take it and then use your illustration to explain how it related to today's material. Within the first two or three minutes, make sure you have stopped talking and make sure at least a half dozen of your students are talking instead. Interject when appropriate, keep it moving, but take the role of guide, rather than of lecturer.

This is the great trap to avoid: Too often, we try to cram six or eight learning objectives into an hour of instruction. Start with three—that's right, three. It will strike fear in your heart as you begin to prepare for the class, but trust me—if you embed three large objectives into each class, and leave time to delve into each with sufficient depth, you'll find yourself less stressed about "getting through all the material" and instead slow down and take a few diversionary dirt roads along the path. We've never had a semester's worth of evaluations without several references to our rambling, and we could not care less, for we designed each and every one.

Here we return to style. Teaching, for us, is a natural extension of our personality: exuberant, enthusiastic, an unabashed geek proudly dispensing knowledge. It makes us happy, and thus it is fun. That may well be the antithesis of your style, and that is perfectly fine. What's important is that you find your comfort point, and embrace it without reservation. It's the honesty that matters. Teaching, at the end of the day, is a culminating process. You build the class, class after class, and you build your style, semester after semester. It has to be an honest version of your pedagogical philosophy, or the students will see through it in a heartbeat. Think, for a moment, of the teachers you adore, and those you loathe—and reflect for a moment about what you loved, and hated, about each. It comes down to style, and that indescribable rapport that the best teachers build and the worst teachers destroy.

Three things simultaneously create your teaching style, and while no one can say with certainty what their teaching style is, there are helpful guides and exercised designed to crystallize thinking. My favorite is adapted from the excellent "Mastering the Teaching of Adults" (1991) and uses five questions to help you identify your teaching style:

1. Why do you believe your students want to learn? Describe them as learners in any way you can.
2. What are your aims for teaching? What do you hope to accomplish when you teach? What do your aims say about you as a teacher?
3. Does your subject matter affect your beliefs about teaching or learning? If so, explain how.
4. Create a list in response to the following prompt: "When I teach . . ." Once you've created the list, reflect on why you do what you do.
5. What do you believe about learning? How would you describe it? What are your sources for your beliefs?

Each of these prompts demands a great deal of self-reflection. Are you setting goals for your teaching, and have you given ample thought to what your students want to know before you teach?

Inspired by these questions, we began a seminar recently by asking students directly: What did they wish to get from the class? They were stunned for a moment by the directness of the question, and surprised by us asking it. The depth of the answers surprised us. Students had definite goals in mind, and while we expected some of them, several were completely unexpected and influenced everything we did the rest of the semester.

This anecdote contains an important realization for us all: More than 25 years later, our teaching style is still changing. It always will. In "The Art of Teaching," Jay Parini explains that the Latin word persona implies that a voice is discovered by "sounding through" a mask. "Most of the successful teachers I know have been deeply aware that their self-presentation involves, or has involved at some point, the donning of a mask," he wrote. "A beginning teacher will have to try on countless masks before finding one that fits, that seems appropriate, that works to organize and embody a teaching voice."

While we find the mask analogy a bit troubling, it's also an honest reflection. No one walks into a classroom without adjusting a bit to the bright lights of the stage. We all affect a style, and the sooner we realize it, the better.

The process of experimenting with various teaching personas or voices, of finding our way to a style that fits comfortably is a process, but the random sampling of styles can be painful and humbling. Most of us start with visions of our most and least favorite teachers, but we try to adopt these preferred ways of teaching without giving much thought to what we might be good at and what we probably shouldn't try.

We'd suggest a starting point for developing a teaching style: You ought to be having fun and be an authentic version of yourself. Anything else is theater, and students loathe teachers who act rather than teach. So we can set forth a few principles as a way of starting to build your classroom persona:

1. **Tell them what you know, admit what you don't know.** Too many new teachers think it's better to bluff their way through material they have not mastered or questions that challenge them. No! Nothing is more destructive. Instead, simply acknowledge that you don't know, go out and find the answer, and bring it to the next session or even shoot the class an email later with an answer. Students warm to the authenticity of the teacher who is untroubled by the fact they don't know everything.

2. **Demonstrate, early on, that failure is part of the process.** This is particularly important in skills courses, where students nervously await criticism from the know-it-all professor. So ease their minds by holding up a piece of student work, explaining how it fell short of the standard, then praise the effort. It's entirely surprising to ask the

class, "How could she have made this sentence more active?" rather than to simply read the sentence and then point out its passive voice. One way criticizes; the other collectivizes instruction and leaves the student with helpful feedback. It also establishes the all-important ground rule that everyone's work will be discussed in class.

3. **Don't be afraid to talk about, well, anything.** Go off script, often. Be willing to embrace the conversational thread and head down a tangent or three. Your students will appreciate your willingness to improvise, and they'll be far more likely to engage with you on the material that matters if you breathe a little life into the class by letting them talk about last night's ball game or a story making its way through the news cycle. Also, make a point to talk about your own life in some way, every class session. Even if it is a brief "this reminds me of . . ." you'll find that students are intensely curious about you, your family, your work experience and the like. So let them in, as much as you're comfortable.

4. **Err on the side of being a human being.** These are college students, at the end of the day, so don't treat them like children. Yes, demand professionalism. But don't assume they know what that entails. You'll often have to articulate why something annoys you rather than simply throw out pronouncements and judgments from the lectern. It's easy, so easy to be the tough teacher, enforcer of all rules, no mercy and all of that. Provided you don't mind not actually teaching anyone anything, and not influencing a single life in a positive way, you'll delight in the certainty of your pronouncements and begin a lot of conversations with your like-minded colleagues by sighing and saying, "Students these days . . ."

   Instead, why not try to empathize a bit. Students today are under a lot of stress. The world is a lot more competitive, and more complex, than the world we grew up in, and college is a pressure cooker filled with anxiety, social climbing and a host of other complications. Students often are balancing a host of issues, working a part-time job and watching their debt load skyrocket. So yeah, maybe their attention span can leave a wee bit to be desired. It gives you the ideal way to . . .

5. **Make all of it fun.** The goal of every class session, for me at least, is to have fun and make the classroom a pleasant place where we can think critically and learn. So if we are staring out at a sea of smartphones, we can either get serious and chide the students, in which case they have completely shut down, or we can turn it into a laughable moment by grabbing our own smartphone and asking everyone what's got everyone so tuned out. One approach intimidates, while the other gets the same message across while we all laugh a bit.

FIELD TRIPS AND GUEST SPEAKERS

Like so many aspects of teaching, field trips and guest speakers can be wonderful in moderation. Used strategically, and interspersed through-out the term, each has its role. Overuse of either can wear thin, and prove to be more work than it's worth.

When planning the course, start with one or two guest speakers, and if appropriate to the course content, an equal number of field trips. The starting point for every such unit should be a review of the learning objectives for the course: Does the guest speaker or field trip help you achieve learning goals?

Some lessons learned along the way:

- Field trips require a fair amount of advance planning. Start early! And keep in mind that some students may face transportation issues, so make sure you've thought through logistics.
- Coordinate with the field trip host to make sure you cover the points you want to stress.
- Bring along a small token of your appreciation for the host. It's a nice touch and makes it easier the next time.
- Take notes during the field trip and encourage students to ask questions beforehand. Prep the students by explaining what they are likely to see and how it relates to class the session before the field trip. Assign a reflective essay following the field trip with some prompted questions, so the students have a reason to engage.

As for guest speakers:

- A week or so before the visit, schedule a chat with the speaker to review what you want them to discuss. Ask whether they have any questions, share a copy of the syllabus and give them some context so they are not coming in unprepared.
- Ask whether they have any audiovisual or technology needs, and ask if they have handouts to prepare beforehand.
- Prepare a brief but informative introduction for the speaker.
- Ensure that parking and other logistics are in place.
- Prepare the students beforehand by brainstorming questions to ask the guest speaker.
- Don't be a passive observer. Facilitate discussion by interjecting, asking questions yourself and heading off rambling discourse so the conversation remains on track.

Like most aspects of teaching, guest speakers and field trips can work, but only if you approach them not as a day off, but as another way to engage students in the class material. Typically, professors may invest weeks of effort into scheduling a guest speaker, but less effort into arranging their classroom activities so that the speaker's appearance will further the curricular objectives of the course. When professors invite guest experts into their classrooms, they tend to conceptualize the arrangement as a compartmentalized event that stands outside of the regular current of class activity. The block of time scheduled for the guest tends to represent a break from the class schedule, rather than an essential part of the course material. As a result, the guest's contributions are not as impactful as they might be if steps were taken to ensure that some degree of alignment were achieved between the curriculum and the speaker.

IN THE TRENCHES

Field Trips Should Be a Learning Experience

Chris Roush, UNC-Chapel Hill

Back in high school, I remember that field trips were a day off from learning for myself and my fellow students, so when I became a university professor, I vowed to turn them into an excursion where students got something out of the experience.

For example, when I taught an Advanced Reporting class for master's students, who spent the semester reporting and writing stories about Blue Cross Blue Shield of North Carolina, I arranged a field trip to the company's headquarters where the students sat in the boardroom and interviewed the chief executive officer. All that took was coordinating with the company's corporate communications staff. The students later said it was the best class that we'd had all semester because none of them had ever had such an experience.

My colleagues who teach multimedia skills have similar field trips to the North Carolina coast, and have even taken students to such exotic locations as the Galapagos Islands and Africa during Spring Break when time permits. If you're planning such a field trip for a class, make sure the students know in advance that they or their parents will have costs associated with the experience.

I like the Spring Break or Fall Break field trip. For years, I would take a group of students to New York for Spring Break, and I organized meetings at the New York Stock Exchange, the Bear Stearns trading floor and at media organizations such as Bloomberg News, the Wall Street Journal and Business-Week magazine. Students were given a schedule and expected to be at each meeting on time. Such a field trip helped the students see in person some of the concepts, such as how the stock market works, we had discussed in class. Each student paid $300 for the trip, and that covered their plane fare and hotel, which was then scheduled by someone at the university. It wasn't a requirement for the class, and rarely did half the class participate. But it was a learning experience for this who did go.

Field trips often depend on your location. It's much easier to plan field trips to newsrooms when you're in or near a major metropolitan area. When I was an undergraduate journalism student, one of my professors took us to visit the University of Alabama-Birmingham, where we met with scientists and doctors and got to talk to the Birmingham News reporter who covered the medical school. That was a two-hour trip both ways, making it a full day, so we missed other classes. Such a field trip requires the patience of your faculty colleagues.

WAYS TO ENCOURAGE PARTICIPATION AND ENGAGEMENT—AND DIVERSIFY THE CONVERSATION!

At the end of the day, we all want to build a classroom environment that encourages critical thinking and deep engagement with the material. We want a vibrant, active culture, one that invites student participation rather than passivity and forced dialogue. Getting there is no simple task, and there are a multitude of ways to encourage the sort of involvement that brings the class to life.

Engaging students in the classroom is a struggle. Getting students from diverse backgrounds to talk is even more difficult. In most classrooms, other than at historically black colleges or urban campuses, the majority of students are white. Ethnic minority students in these classes usually refrain from engaging in discussion, unless prodded by the professor. There are other students in the room as well who make a conscious effort not to be heard. If the class is a large lecture, they may feel intimidated by the size, or shy about talking in public or believe that their comments will not be valued by classmates or the instructor. What they do not understand is that the diversity of cultures, thoughts and perspectives bring value to the educational process. It is important for teachers to recognize that value and help students feel comfortable engaging in the classroom conversations.

To facilitate open conversations that engage as many students as possible, instructors need to embrace the diversity in the room. Students come in all shapes and sizes and from all walks of life. What you see on the surface is not who they are when they engage in conversation. There are several ways to determine the diversity of a class. One suggestion is to ask the class to write a paragraph or two describing their high school. Another assignment is to have them document their social interactions for a week, but do not tell them why until after they turn it in. There are others you can come up with. The goal is to identify the various forms of diversity within a class. Doing so can lead to further ideas on how to engage students in classroom conversations.

When engaging students in classroom conversations, especially when the goal is to have a diversity of opinions and ideas, it is important to set some ground rules. One is that no one, not even the instructor, has the right to talk over the person who is talking. That is just disrespectful and can stifle the diverse discussion you are trying to achieve. Another is to try and suspend judgement. That is a tough one. As Keith Woods, chief of diversity for National Public Radio and former dean of faculty at the Poynter Institute, points out, when someone makes a statement, those listening will first perceive what was said, then judge the motives of the individual, then attribute those motives based on little information. Instructors should constantly remind students to seek further information before making judgement. It will require asking more questions that will lead to more conversation, which is necessary to get a diversity of voices.

One of the main obstacles to fostering diverse conversations is fear. To quote Jedi Master Yoda, "Fear is the path to the dark side." Some people will say that they do not care what others think, but in reality they do. In the classroom, this plays out all the time. The instructor will make a statement or pose a question and there is silence in the room. It is called fear. Some students will choose to remain ignorant about a subject rather than ask a question in front of their peers. This is when instructors need to own the room. It is imperative that you help students acknowledge the fear and break through barriers that impede knowledge. One way to do this is to allow students to ask you a difficult question and be willing to answer it, within reason. Once students get a sense that you are willing to be open, they are more likely to relax. It is also effective later when there is silence in the room during a difficult discussion. Just saying "fear in the room" can trigger students to engage in conversation to seek answers they otherwise would not get.

Woods has several additional suggestions for constructive conversation in diverse environments. The first is to be honest. This relates to our previous discussion about fear. Fear can keep students from saying what they actually mean. Clear and concise language leaves little doubt about meaning and can instill trust and understanding.

Second, seek clarification. It is important to ask questions before judging and making conclusions. Don't assume you understand what someone is saying. Ask the person, "What do you mean?" This can lead to a more meaningful and authentic conversation that can draw in students because they will see that they will be given an opportunity to clarify any statements they make.

Next, instructors and students should challenge with passion, not poison. Those who are talking should be allowed to make their statements without interruption. They should also be given the opportunity to clarify their statements. That does not mean they should not be challenged on what they say. This can and should be done respectfully and with the understanding that in the end all parties may agree to disagree. That does not mean there is no understanding. There is also an opportunity to gain knowledge, which is the goal of every class discussion.

Entering a conversation with an open mind is **very** important, especially in our profession. We cannot be militant in our ignorance. There are no guarantees in honest conversations. If students are to learn, they must be willing to change their minds. They also must be willing to stay in the room when the conversation gets heated. A student seeking answers to questions may not always be comfortable with the response. The person responding to the questions may not provide answers in a delightful tone. Honesty and candor sometimes are not sugar and spice. However, if everyone agrees to stay in the room and be respectful, there can be meaningful conversation and instruction.

CONCLUSION

It might seem a tad simplistic to conclude by saying that it's all about the attitude—but it's all about the attitude, bolstered by more than a little strategy. Building a classroom that students want to come to takes time, planning and effort, but more than any one thing, it takes enthusiasm, a willingness to experiment and a sense of play. Unburdening yourself enough to be free in the classroom is an endless process. It's painful for some to unveil that sort of vulnerability in front of a group of strangers, and it's often threatening to humble yourself before a group of students, but it's also the first step toward building a meaningful rapport.

Maybe the best way to approach teaching is to reverse engineer the process. Start by thinking about what you want a group of students to describe you as years later: "Professor X was . . ." and then build the sort of classroom that generates those sorts of descriptions. It will take years of honing, and you'll encounter setbacks along the way. But oh, on those days when it all works, when the students eagerly engage, when they challenge you and one another . . . well, it simply doesn't get any better than that.

SAMPLE EXERCISE:
ENGAGING DIVERSITY IN HIGHER EDUCATION

Gather in groups of five for a discussion about the use of the ACT or SAT for admissions at your institution. Should it factor as much as it does in the admission decision? How much should the high school GPA be weighed? What about prospective student's high school rank? How do race and socioeconomics factor into the decision? During the conversation remember the keys to having a difficult conversation discussed in this chapter, especially judgment and staying in the room. The group must agree on what will be presented to the rest of the class.

REFERENCES

Apps, J. (1991). Mastering the Teaching of Adults. Malabar, FL: Krieger Publishing Co.

Lang, J. M. (January 11, 2016). Small Changes in Teaching: The First 5 Minutes of Class. The Chronicle of Higher Education. http://www.chronicle.com/article/Small-Changes-in-Teaching-The/234869

Len-Rios, M. and Perry, E., eds. (2016). Cross-Cultural Journalism: Communicating Strategically About Diversity. New York: Routledge.

Parini, J. (2005). The Art of Teaching. New York: Oxford University Press.

5

Exercises and Projects

Mary T. Rogus, Ohio University

Think back to a time when you were trying to master a new skill that looked so easy when others did it, but you couldn't seem to get it. A graduate student tells a classic story of this frustration. She worked part-time as a waitress at a family-owned Chinese restaurant and was asked to help make wonton noodles after her lunch shift. She watched as the family members, including a 10-year-old daughter, nimbly folded pasta squares around a small piece of meat in such a way that they didn't fall apart when boiled. The family watched with surprise and then humor as the young woman tried repeatedly, day after day, to properly fold the wonton noodles.

It was years later when that young woman stepped into a classroom and tried to teach students the job she had done for nearly 20 years that she finally understood why she couldn't learn how to make wonton noodles. The family members in the restaurant had done it so long, they weren't conscious of the steps to folding the pasta. It was one continuous, quick motion that none of them could break down for the woman trying to learn.

USING YOUR PROFESSIONAL
EXPERIENCE IN THE CLASSROOM

Professional experience is one of the most valuable things an instructor brings into the classroom. But knowing how to do something and how to teach others to do it are two extremely different skills.

Think about where the students are when they come into your class. Chances are that for most skills classes, students know what the final product should look or sound like. They're in a consumer mentality. Your job is to get them into a producer mentality. So start with the final product and backward engineer.

Take a mental tour of your process when you created a news story or put together a press packet or developed a strategy to capture an audience, and then document it. That step-by-step process is how you'll share your experience with the students in a way that they can learn the process. Make sure that at each step you connect with the final product so the students understand how it fits in the process of learning the skill.

Table 5.1 shows an example of how a former television news producer turned two major steps of her daily producing process and handling breaking news into weeks of a "TV News Producing" class.

WAR STORIES VS. CASE STUDIES

If you've spent any time working professionally in journalism or strategic communication, you probably have a lot of those "you'll never believe what happened to me" stories. Students love war stories, and they are great for establishing your credibility. But many a new instructor who comes directly from the newsroom into the classroom makes the mistake of getting caught up in the students' eagerness to hear all about their experiences on the job. The problem is students can't learn *how* to do something from your stories of what you did or accomplished, and don't expect them to take away the same lessons you learned from your mistakes or happy accidents. Be selective with your war stories to emphasize a point or provide an example after you've already broken down the skill into its step-by-step components as discussed above.

There is one excellent pedagogical use of your personal and professional experiences, and that's developing case studies. Case studies are especially effective if you're teaching a concept or theory class such as media ethics or communication law. Students need to not only learn the concepts but also know how to apply them in making decisions. When you create case studies for students to analyze, they learn from your experiences because they're not just told what happened, but are challenged to make their own decisions based on the same facts, questions and dilemmas you faced. They like knowing they are working on real problems they might face on the job, and your personal connection gives them "behind the scenes" information about the final outcome. Certainly, there are many existing banks of case studies for most classes, but students respond to the sense of being an insider that your personal experiences can give them.

Table 5.1. TV News Producing

Step	Skills/Knowledge Needed	Lessons	Exercises
Choosing stories for the day	What's important/ relevant to your audience; target market for show; background knowledge of local, state, national, world news, culture, sports, weather, etc.	Where/how to research your community; choosing/angling stories for your target audience; developing a daily news/info diet	Listening Post: Choose a community gathering spot, eavesdrop, develop a story proposal from what people are talking about. Target Audience: Student groups get "market cards" and from the information about their target market, they find five today stories for a 5 p.m. newscast.
Building the newscast rundown	Computer program ENPS (Electronic News Producing System) Critical connection between rundown and what gets on TV Story flow and pacing, anchor blocking, use of graphics	Technical operation of ENPS system and rundown layout Nearly everyone working on your newscast should be able to do their job from only the rundown Concepts of info processing and how connections between stories (flow) helps, how to assign anchors to aid flow and performance, types of graphics and concepts of graphic use to aid info processing	Practice Rundown: Each student has their own practice rundown in ENPS and every exercise is done in that rundown. Backward Engineering: Students watch a newscast and story by story create the rundown that would have led to that show on the air. Story Flow/Pacing: Multiple exercises with lists of stories to create a first block of a local newscast. With each practice exercise, a new element (i.e., anchor blocking, graphics, writing, etc.) is added until students are producing a complete rundown.
Breaking news	Quick decision-making, prioritizing information, communicating, is it really news?	How you can "prepare" for breaking news, deploying resources and keeping people on task, control room— communicating and managing live, unscripted TV	Breaking News War Games: Students groups set up coverage for a news day with given set of stories and resources. "Chance Cards" give each group advantages/disadvantages. Move to real time with constant updates on major breaking news story— students decide what to tweet, cut-in on air, how to adjust their newscasts. Major story twist at the end.

MEDIA ETHICS CASE STUDY FROM ACTUAL EXPERIENCE

Graphic Video/Diversity Case

The following is a case study of a real story that presents multiple ethical and practical challenges. Assume you are the executive producer in this newsroom, required to plan the way the story is going to be covered for the 10 p.m. newscast the night the story breaks and the next day's follow-ups. Detail in your conclusion what you would and would not put on TV and why.

The City:
Green Bay, Wisconsin
  Major Industries: paper mills, lumber, dairy farming
  Major Stories: Green Bay Packers, outdoor activities, environmental issues, education, Native American gambling, Native American culture and treaty issues, Asian culture
  Minorities: Oneida Native American Tribe, Hmong Community (natives of Laos—largest Hmong community in the United States.) Both minority groups are very isolated in the Green Bay area, keeping to themselves with very little interaction with the community at large unless there is a clash of cultures.

The Story:
The Los Angeles headquarters of the extreme animal rights group PETA (People for the Ethical Treatment of Animals) calls your news director and tells him PETA has an undercover videotape it made showing a local kennel owner shooting a dog and selling it to a young Asian couple to be used for food. PETA is bringing the tape to Green Bay and would like to work with a local TV station to expose this kennel owner. PETA promises to provide access to the couple who made the tape and not to give the tape to any other station. In return, PETA asks the station to set up a meeting with the local district attorney to view the tape.

  Your news director agrees with the provision that the station is given the name of the kennel owner, so he/she can be checked out prior to PETA's arrival with the tape. PETA provides the name, and the kennel owner is researched, along with laws regarding animal treatment. Research shows that the kennel owner is licensed to sell, but not breed, dogs, and is licensed to provide dogs to the University of Wisconsin for medical research. He typically picks up strays as his source of animals. He is not licensed to sell any animal meat for human consumption, and must kill the animals humanely if sold to the university. He must keep the animals clean and well fed until they are sold. You also find out that there was an animal cruelty case against this kennel owner seven years ago, but the charges were ultimately dismissed. In the course of covering that case, a videographer from your station had an altercation with the kennel owner, which ended in damaged camera equipment, and injury to the videographer. The station sued the kennel owner for $50,000 in damages and the case was settled out of court for $25,000.

PETA brings the undercover videotape to the station and it shows an Asian couple (woman pregnant, man with a cast on his arm, which is where the camera is hidden) talking to the kennel owner, then the kennel owner brings a dog out of a cage, shoots it, wraps it up in butcher paper and loads the package into the couple's car trunk. There is no audio. No blood is seen, but you do see the dog shot and then it falls. PETA explains that an Asian couple was chosen because that reinforced the cultural stereotype in Wisconsin that the Hmong community regularly eats dog meat, and PETA thought they would be believed.

The day after PETA arrives (now three days from the original phone call) a meeting is set for 3 p.m. with the county district attorney. Your reporter and photographer are allowed to attend. The district attorney looks at the video and completely unexpectedly issues a warrant to immediately remove all animals from the kennel owner's farm. By 4 p.m., Humane Society workers are taking dozens of dogs off the farm and describe the conditions in which the animals are living as disgusting and inhumane. By 7 p.m., 180 dogs have been removed from the farm and the kennel owner is charged with dozens of counts of cruelty to animals.

You have the entire story exclusively—but because of the raid on the farm and the charges filed, you know the story won't stay exclusive beyond that night. You have to break the story on the 10 p.m. news, even though you had expected to have several more days to plan your coverage. No other media outlet will ever have the undercover video of the dog being shot, or the video of the raid on the kennel and removal of the animals.

For Instructors: Ethical Issues/Station Resolution
> *Truth*—video has no audio, undercover video, not shot by the station; speed vs. accuracy of breaking news
> *Minimize Harm*—racial stereotyping of Hmong people by using Asian couple in undercover video; graphic nature of video showing dog being killed
> *Conflict of Interest*—past altercation and lawsuit with kennel owner
> *Independence*—setting up meeting with district attorney for PETA in return for exclusive access to undercover video

At 10 p.m.:
- Live reporter story from Humane Society shelter where dogs were kept telling story of raid—for transparency acknowledged that station helped set up meeting between PETA and district attorney that led to raid
- Dog-shooting video narrated by Asian couple—anchor warning before video that it showed dog getting shot; clearly acknowledged PETA as source and that there was no audio (station never ran video again until it was played at trial)

- Asian couple on camera explaining why they agreed to go undercover despite stereotype, and confirmation from Hmong community leader that Hmong don't eat dog meat.
- For transparency and context, story about past charges against kennel owner that were dropped, and station history with kennel owner

Next Day:
- Anchor voiceover of kennel owner in court
- Reporter story recapping raid and follow-up on dogs
- Long-form reporter story with Hmong Community Center about cultural myths and reaction to use of Asian couple by PETA

LEARNING FROM OUR MISTAKES

While students may not always get the message when we *tell* about our personal experiences, we can *show* them. When trying to show students what's expected or desired in a project, we usually choose good examples, especially if we're sharing our own work. Sally Ann Cruikshank teaches video and audio storytelling at Middle Tennessee State University and finds that sometimes the worst examples are better teaching tools. She says it's interesting to watch students react to a bad example of whatever skill she's teaching after several good examples. Usually one or two students will try to find something good to say about it, thinking she wouldn't show it if it wasn't a good example, then one brave student will let loose on why he or she thinks it's bad, and the rest follow suit. Being able to recognize the results of mistakes in a final product, before they go out and try it, provides a more concrete reason to avoid those mistakes. And again, you are making the connection for students between an individual skill and the final content they'll produce.

Another professor who teaches the introductory writing and reporting course shows his classes some of his former students' first stories (with their permission) including his comments and grade and then reveals the stories they're writing now for The Washington Post, New York Times, CNN and other major news outlets. He says it softens the blow of giving back that first writing assignment. Another twist on this idea is to share with students some of your first work from college or your first job. Providing aspirational examples gives students a goal, but seeing early work from the time when you were where they are gives them hope that they can get there, and usually provides a little humor.

BRINGING IN LEARNING PARTNERS

Learning partnerships can be a great way to foster professional relationships formed through faculty and companies, and are an ideal way to formalize outreach and service through a class.

A learning partnership can be as informal as an invitation for a corporate executive to get involved with a class by dropping in a few times throughout the semester, or as formal as a memorandum of understanding and the endowing of a class or program in exchange for a course dedicated to a corporate project. Partnerships in which a company "embeds" in a class are a wonderful way to get real-world lessons into your classroom, and corporate leaders simply love being around students and imparting wisdom learned on the job.

This can take many different forms. A public relations class can work to develop press packets for companies. An advertising class can produce campaigns for government organizations. A journalism class can cover local school boards or other government bodies for local media that no longer have the time or resources to do so. The partnership can even be broader. At UNC-Chapel Hill, an advanced business journalism class created the North Carolina Business News Wire, and their stories were sent out to media statewide each day. Some of those stories were then published online for media such as The Charlotte Observer, The (Durham) Herald-Sun and WRALTechWire.com.

Partnerships can be as flexible as your creativity, and that of your administrators, allows. For example, what if you developed a partnership with a local business to bring in speakers throughout the semester to mentor students? The company could promise a set number of mentors to work on resume development and career skills, and in exchange, you could have the class work on researching and presenting solutions to a business problem facing the company. Our classes are filled with millennials—and corporate America is puzzled about how to market to this crucial demographic. So make your class a living research and development lab.

Your students are the stronger for the partnerships, and faculty are enriched by continual collaboration with professionals in the disciplines for which we prepare students to lead. Universities are an unmatched site of creativity and innovation. When we put students, faculty and professionals together, useful ideas and knowledge for journalism, business, the arts and the public good multiply.

The key is to identify a need that the business has, and then build the classroom experience around working with the partner to provide a solution. Partnerships can yield experiential learning, internships and other forms of corporate support, and they open career pathways for students. The starting point is conversation: Visit local businesses germane to your discipline and spend time getting to know alumni of your program in those businesses. You'll find them eager to give back, and learning partnerships are an ideal way to involve them.

Let me give you an example: At UNC-Chapel Hill's School of Media and Journalism, a design class works with local small businesses and non-profit organizations each semester. The students meet with representatives at the beginning of the semester to learn about their goals and needs. By the end of the semester, the students will have developed logos and color schemes for the businesses and organizations to use on their websites, their business cards and other materials. It's a service that many of these businesses and organizations can't afford, and they probably don't have the time to spend on developing a logo themselves because they're too busy running their day-to-day operation.

Here is another example that used data journalism: When the Scripps School of Journalism at Ohio University wanted to develop a data journalism class, the school director approached an alum at The Columbus Dispatch who was managing editor overseeing special projects about a partnership. At the time, the Dispatch was developing reporting projects from an extensive database on the economy, politics and culture of the Appalachian region of Southeast Ohio, where Ohio University is located. The newspaper agreed to provide students full access to the data and send reporters, data analysts and editors every two weeks to guide the students and professor through reporting projects. While learning how to find and report stories from a massive database, the students also did some of the legwork for Dispatch reporters, getting the personal stories that brought the data to life. When the paper put out its special section on Appalachia Ohio, several of the students' projects were part of it.

USING THE CAMPUS LIBRARY

As members of the journalism or strategic communication profession, we know that practically every job or individual task our students will do contributes to the communication of information to an audience. As educators, with virtually unlimited production techniques and distribution channels for those messages, we spend most of our time teaching the who, what, when, where, why and how of communicating that information. Sometimes, the important process of gathering and critically analyzing that information gets less attention than it should. With the "Google = research" and "Wikipedia is a primary source" mindset of students, that part of the journalism process is more important than ever. Your campus library and community public libraries can be great partners for breaking that mindset.

The old notion of shoe-leather reporting is just that, old. You're more likely to get carpel tunnel syndrome than wear out a pair of shoes working in the digital information world. But the one advantage of those days, when the only ways to get information were talking to people or searching through paper documents and microfilm archives, was you always knew the source of your information. Reference librarians are information source experts, and they're typically eager and enthusiastic about sharing that expertise.

Many campus library systems have subject area reference librarians who can do workshops on finding primary source information, and working with government and other public databases. They will work with you to design exercises specific to the type of research students will need to do for your class. For example, Ohio University's communication reference librarian Jessica Hagman introduced students in a "TV News Election Coverage" class to a series of databases that collected and organized election finance data. She designed an exercise in which students integrated and cross-referenced information from three of those databases to create campaign funding profiles for our local state legislative candidates. She also created a research resource webpage for the class that had links to more than a dozen helpful websites and databases for election coverage, as well as tutorials for the students to learn to use them effectively.

Likewise, the reference librarian at the Athens, Ohio, public library pointed the students in the right direction to research local tax levies and ballot issues, including terminology (such as what's a "mill"?) and voting history on past levies. In one two-and-a-half-hour class session, the students knew where to find all the background they needed for long-form television stories on key Athens County tax levies, plus do data journalism on where the major out-of-state campaign funding was coming from—all using primary sources.

The other area of expertise that reference librarians can help with is information literacy, which in our social media fake news frenzy has never been more vital. Students are often shocked when a reference librarian reveals the true sources of information or pictures and video they chose as most credible from a typical Google search. Another exercise valuable for learning research and sourcing is editing a Wikipedia page. Have the students choose a short Wikipedia entry for a topic they're interested in and then fact check and source every piece of information on that page, correcting any errors, or even create their own fully-researched page. The Wikimedia Foundation has an extensive education program, and Executive Director Katherine Maher says the Foundation is anxious to work with educators on Wikipedia projects. For more information, go to: https://wikimediafoundation.org/wiki/Wikipedia_Education_Program.

INCORPORATING RESEARCH
EXERCISES INTO NON-RESEARCH CLASSES

Much of the research data strategic communication and journalism practitioners use is collected by someone else, either in-house by a research department or contracted out to professional researchers, such as the audience and consumer research company Nielsen. It's important not only for students to know how to find that research, read it and communicate it an understandable way, but they also should know something about how it's collected.

Undergraduate media research courses typically review the various methodologies for collecting data, but students don't always get to actually conduct a survey, a focus group or perform content analysis. An easy way to give them that hands-on experience without having to design their own studies is to get them involved in research projects you or your colleagues are working on. Find out who in your department is currently collecting data for a study, and see if they would be willing to train your students to participate in that data collection.

There also are ways to include small research projects in other classes. For example, in a copywriting class, have the students test various lines of copy with small focus groups of the target audience—it could be members of a student organization or sorority, a church group or a neighborhood association. In a journalism history class, have students dig into the historical collections at your library and write a short biography using original letters, documents and reports, or track down old letters and documents from family archives (or attics), and do the same for a family member two or more generations back. In a news reporting or broadcast news class, bring home the message about diversity by having students conduct a content analysis of local television newscasts to determine the racial diversity of sources and source roles in stories, using their perceptions (just as viewers would do) of the on-camera sources' race. It's eye-opening when students find, as they do repeatedly with this exercise, that most of the officials and experts in stories are white males, and most of the crime victims or suspects are ethnic minorities.

In these examples, the instructors developed the focus-group protocol, showed students how to find and use archival material and designed the content analysis codebook, but the students did the data collection and very simple summary analysis. More importantly, they discovered for themselves message impact, primary source history and the impact of not consciously paying attention to diversity in sourcing.

INCORPORATING INTERNATIONAL
AND MULTICULTURAL EXERCISES INTO CLASSES

Most of the content that our students produce, both while in college and on the job, will be targeted toward a local or regional audience. However, most of their distribution platforms will be global. Any content produced for or redistributed on the web or social media can be accessed by audiences around the world. And many of those "local" audiences are made up of different cultures. It's important that students think about the multiple ways the same message might be perceived by different cultures and communities.

An example of differing international perspectives on a news philosophy in America caught a faculty member totally by surprise during visual storytelling workshops in the Middle East and Southeast Asia. Shortly after the U.S. invasion of Iraq, she was bombarded with questions asking why television journalists in America supported President Bush in their Iraq war stories. Shocked, she asked why they thought that, and the unanimous answer was, "You don't show any bodies on TV." Most of the journalists in these countries faced government censorship at some level, and so their perception was that decisions not to show bodies of U.S. soldiers or Iraqis had to be the result of some government coercion, rather than a sensitivity for the audience.

One of the easiest exercises to get students starting to think about the lenses different cultures might perceive messages through is to do some comparative analysis. Take the same story or the same product, have students find international English language versions of that story or advertisements for that product and then analyze the similarities and differences. A similar exercise can be done comparing mainstream and multicultural media within the U.S. Victoria LaPoe, who is Native American and researches Native American media, had students in an introductory reporting class do that for coverage of the Dakota pipeline protests near the Standing Rock reservation. Students were first surprised to find out there *were* Native American newspapers and news websites, and secondly were amazed by the differences in sourcing, descriptive word choices and visual images.

Another exercise that can help students understand international or multicultural perspectives is to do local reaction stories, or create local support messages for some international event. But instead of the typical approach of trying to find someone from your campus or community who happens to be on the scene, look for sources from the country in your community. Talk to them and then take the next step and have them connect you with a local source on the ground in-country. Do a Skype or WhatsApp interview. Most colleges have students and faculty from across the globe—find them and tell the story or design a message of support from their perspective.

STUDENT MEDIA AND AGENCIES

In-class exercises and projects are the ways we teach skills and concepts. But they are typically one-time experiences, whether it's a single in-class exercise or a semester-long project for a capstone or campaigns class. Students need opportunities to practice and perfect what they learn in classes, as well as focus it on their specific goals and interest areas. That's where student media and student PR/advertising agencies can be invaluable supplements to our academic curriculum. They give students the opportunity to experience their future jobs and careers from the ground up, usually starting with assistant-level jobs and growing into leadership positions, working with real clients and audiences, in an ongoing relationship. Your role as faculty advisor is key to successful learning in these outside organizations. It's also important to remember that advising student media and agencies, while rewarding and fun, can be very time consuming and, in some schools, may not count for much in your performance evaluations for salary increases, promotion or tenure.

THE STUDENT PR/ADVERTISING AGENCY

Often student-run public relations and/or advertising agencies start as subgroups of a Public Relations Student Society of America (PRSSA) or American Advertising Federation (AAF) student chapter. They might also start with participation in the AAF's National Student Advertising Competition or PRSSA's Bateman Case Study competition. Both are national competitions in which students work on a full campaign for a sponsoring client. Many schools use the competitions as the basis for their advertising and PR campaigns classes. But whether students participate as part of a class or independently, they get the opportunity to operate as an agency, serving a client. While all students do all tasks in intermediate skills classes, working with a client to create an entire campaign lets them focus on their areas of strength and interest, be it strategy, research, copywriting or creative. Moving forward from participating in National Student Advertising Competition (NSAC) or Bateman competitions to developing an in-house agency gives students the added experience of pitching, developing and maintaining client relationships.

Here are some things that as an advisor for a student ad or PR agency you can do to make sure the students develop successful and professional relationships with clients, and enhance their portfolios without becoming slave labor:

- **Help manage resources:** One of the quickest ways for a student agency to fail is to take on more clients than it can handle, or expect that the student who is a whiz at copywriting or can do social media in her sleep can work on three or four client accounts at the same time. Impress on student managers that no account should be pitched unless there's a full staff ready to do the work on that account. Make sure students have clearly defined staff positions with responsibilities and time commitment laid out.
- **Vetting clients:** You probably want to make it a proviso of your agreement to advise a student PR or advertising agency that you will have a role in the vetting of potential clients. This helps keep the students from getting in over their heads, and you can help manage expectations by focusing the students on clients who understand that no matter how professional the students may seem, they are still students. You can also help the students avoid producing campaigns that might be non-complementary with a college or university marketing strategy, or undercutting local PR, advertising and marketing businesses. Have students start with accounts on campus, perhaps even working with the university communication and marketing department, almost as a subcontractor. Look for student organizations that need help publicizing events or student media trying to increase audience. When the student agency is ready to reach out to clients outside campus, direct them to nonprofits or government agencies that need help getting a message out. Also reach out to clients where alumni work, or clients that have been learning partners, as described previously. Avoid companies or organizations simply looking for free labor to do grunt work or function as interns.
- **Responsibility to client:** Work with account supervisors to impress on all students working on any client account that they have a professional responsibility to that client. Make sure students negotiate a contract for services to be rendered with each client. Remind students that those responsibilities must be met according to that contract, even during midterms and finals or sorority/fraternity rush week. Help them understand there's no difference between a contract with their school or department, or a fellow student organization, and a contract with an outside nonprofit or commercial client.
- **There's no such thing as free:** Most clients of student advertising or PR firms choose to work with students because they have no budget for any communications, advertising or marketing. It's one more thing the owner/director/manager adds to his or her plate. So

students who present a professional looking pitch, have training in these areas and are willing to work for the experience can be quite attractive. You, as an advisor, need to make sure the students don't pitch their services as completely free. Make sure the costs of supplies, printing and any media buys get included in every client pitch. Otherwise your department, your students or even you could end up paying these costs out of pocket if they're not part of a contract for services. As your student firm develops a reputation for professional and successful work with off-campus clients, you might even start to ask for a small fee or donation that could support your PRSSA or AAF student chapter, provide promotional materials and cover the cost of pitches for the agency or even support a scholarship.

- **It's all about results:** Emphasize to the students that in the end the client wants one thing—results to the bottom line (whatever that is). The client doesn't want to know how many times you tweeted or how clever your 140 characters were; they want to know how many people clicked through to their website. They don't care how many likes you got on Facebook; they want to know how many of those people actually donated to their cause or showed up for their event. Make sure that right up front in any client pitch and campaign development, account managers are thinking about the metrics of success—how they'll be measured and reported. If they learn nothing else from working on an account except how to calculate and report success in the client's terms, your student PR/advertising agency will have given them a most valuable skill for their future.

ImPRessions is the national award-winning student public relations firm at Ohio University's Scripps School of Journalism. Take a look at its website https://www.ouimpressions.com/ and Facebook page https://www.facebook.com/ouimpressions/ to get an idea of how it's organized, who its clients are and what the students are getting out of the experience.

THE STUDENT NEWSROOM

Student newsrooms provide journalism students with similar opportunities to get quasi-professional experience like strategic communication students get with in-house PR and advertising agencies. In most cases the students are producing content that is distributed to real audiences. The organization and level of university/faculty involvement vary widely, from fully independent student-run newsrooms to faculty/staff supervised, student volunteer newsrooms to faculty-led practicum classes that operate as newsrooms. Most universities have some of each. These newsrooms can be platform focused or converged, but in most, students produce content across multiple platforms. So your involvement with student newsrooms at your university might be minimal, such as serving as an advisor for a student media outlet, or all-encompassing if you teach a practicum class that produces a magazine, news website and/or television newscast.

No matter what your level of involvement with student media, there are some things you can do, or encourage student managers to do, that will enhance their experience, and help build their portfolios:

- **Set and keep deadlines:** Students who learn that deadlines are as inflexible as concrete in journalism will do much better in a professional newsroom. Whether their content goes out daily, weekly, monthly or once a semester, set firm deadlines or encourage student managers to do it for each step of the production process. Then make sure there are serious consequences for missing a deadline, because on the job they could get fired.
- **Teach and model professionalism:** It can be especially difficult for students in managerial roles in the newsroom because they're managing their peers. Clearly defining those roles and modeling professional interactions with student editors and producers can help. Don't assume students understand how to interact professionally, via email, phone or in person with those in the community. Keep attuned for signs of harassment, no matter how "joking" comments or behavior might have been intended. Watch social media for postings that would violate most professional newsroom policies.
- **But remember they're not professionals yet:** The more involved with a student newsroom you are, the more you want the content produced to be excellent, especially when it's going out to a public audience. That desire brings on a tendency to over-edit and stop/fix every potential mistake. There's a fine line between editing for potential libel errors or grammar and completely re-writing because a student didn't use the best broadcast style or narrative format. Students won't produce the same quality content you could after 10 years in the profession. But they will get better with each story they write or layout they produce. It's not a reflection on your teaching or advising if the journalism product is not perfect!
- **Feedback, feedback, feedback:** Your most valuable contribution to any student newsroom is feedback. Make sure the staff is holding regular critique sessions after content is published or aired, and help them to be specific with praise and critical in a constructive way. Students tend not to want to be critical of their peers, but meaningful praise and constructive suggestions for improvement are taken to

heart when they come from student colleagues. Find time for one-on-one feedback—edit a story with the student at your side, review layouts or rundowns with the designer or producer in person, watch a newscast with the student anchor or reporter and give a personal performance critique. If you are teaching a practicum class, use detailed rubrics that give students feedback that is as objective as possible to understand their grade. Whenever possible bring in outside professionals, especially alums, to join critique sessions. Despite your own years of professional experience, sometimes students have to hear improvement suggestions from a person who might hire them before they actually listen. Plus, the professionals' exposure to the good work students produce in realistic newsroom settings helps them to understand we really are training journalists for the real world!

CONCLUSION: THE MORE, THE BETTER

The bottom line, as you're thinking about and designing the exercises and projects that allow your students to do the things you teach, is make the student work as realistic as possible. Instead of writing their own obituary in that introductory news writing course, choose real people in your community whom they have to research. Instead of practicing interviews on each other, send them out to do man-on-the-street interviews. Instead of a sheet of information to write a press release, choose a Facebook event page for a real, upcoming event. Even these simplest of first assignments can be more realistic for students.

Whenever possible use real client problems and case studies for student exercises, and have their work distributed to real audiences. If there's not a student or local media outlet that would publish or air class work that it deems good enough, create your own class blog. Instead of readings quizzes or response papers, a media ethics professor has students blog about the readings. Not only do students get experience producing content online, but in the eight years since the blog was established, there have been more than 250,000 page views from across the country and internationally.

Create real-world working conditions for exercises and projects. If a reporter's first draft would go right to air or online with minimal editing, grade students on that first draft. If there likely would be multiple edits, send the student's work back for revisions, and grade each one. Hold students to deadlines—no excuses. There are few jobs in journalism or strategic communication that don't live and die by deadlines. Try to create as many "real-time" exercises for students as possible. They can't learn to handle a breaking news story or a crisis management situation if they don't ever have the chance to experience it, even in a mock exercise.

And finally, pay attention to and provide feedback on the process of working on and completing exercises and projects, as well as the final product. Most of the learning takes place in the process. Going back to where we started with this chapter, make sure students understand the steps and requirements that get them to the final product, whether it's a 140-character tweet or a semester-long campaign strategy.

6

Taking Your Class Online

Leslie-Jean Thornton, Arizona State University, and Susan Keith, Rutgers University

These days, classes are as likely to take place with physical walls as without them—online. They may be exclusively online, taking place within a managed system; some may have components that bring students and teachers together for in-depth sessions. Other classes, especially those that work best with in-person supervision, may keep with the traditional classroom format but include multiple ways of meeting or presenting work online, or actively work toward creating an understanding of online communication and dynamics.

In this chapter, we'll cover the range, starting with online and blended classes. We have two "guests" with tips, from their own experiences, about making connections and building one's own confidence in a new genre. We will also offer advice about extending any kind of class into the online environment.

USING BLENDED AND ONLINE TEACHING METHODS

Courses offered fully or partly online are growing in popularity at many colleges and universities. The U.S. Department of Education data show that in fall 2014 some 5.8 million postsecondary students were taking at least one course via what is sometimes called "distance education," and 14 percent of students were taking all their classes that way.

In many ways, that's not surprising, as online courses can make sense for students, professors and administrators. Taking courses that are fully or partly online lets students "time-shift" learning from typical daytime or early evening hours to times that better allow them to intern, work or care for children. Teaching an online course can allow professors with long commutes to reduce the time they spend on the road and help those who need to travel for research or to care for aging parents fulfill their teaching duties. Scheduling online courses can help administrators struggling to find classroom space on overcrowded campuses and help schools in rural areas attract professional adjuncts from larger cities.

This suggests that in the future more instructors will be teaching online—including some who may not have sought out the opportunity and others who simply don't know where to start. This section offers advice in six key areas.

Defining the course: The first thing a professor needs to do before signing up to teach online is to determine what that means. At most colleges and universities, "teaching online" refers to delivering a course via the web asynchronously, allowing students to devote time to the subject when and where they like. At some schools, however, "teaching online" refers to having an instructor in one geographical location use technology to deliver course content in real time to students in another place or places. The goals of the two types of course delivery are different, of course, with the latter more closely duplicating face-to-face classroom instruction and the former offering more avenues for blowing up traditional teaching models.

An instructor contemplating teaching online also needs to consider whether the entire course, or only portions of it, will be offered online. Some universities offer courses—often referred to as "blended" or "hybrid" courses—that meet in person for some part of the term and online for some part of the term. One common arrangement, at colleges and universities where many in-person courses meet twice a week, is to have hybrid courses meet once per week in a classroom and then do group or individual work online in lieu of the other course meeting. Another approach to hybrid or blended courses is to meet face to face for some part of the semester and online the rest.

Planning the course: Whichever type of online course a professor teaches, preparation is the key to a successful semester. It's almost impossible for an instructor to sit down in mid-August, throw together a syllabus with some wiggle room and lots of "TBAs" and produce a strong online experience for herself or her students. Instead, there must be an investment in developing the structure of the course, organizing the readings, putting together the assignments, determining the grading rubrics and recording any online lectures. Once all that work is finished, the instructor then generally faces a further—and sometimes daunting—step: doing the click-by-click data entry to create the course structure in a course management system.

Course management systems such as Blackboard, Canvas, Sakai and eCollege are rooted in an era when the internet was largely text-based, as some might argue it still is. (Indeed, when the author of this section of the chapter began teaching online in 2004, the only way for a Mac user to insert a still image into the content management system her university used was to hand-code the HTML!) Although course management systems have improved markedly over the past 10 years, the default mechanism for telling students to do something remains text. Even if the first thing a professor want students to do in a module is watch a video, the most efficient way to get that idea across is probably to use words, placing on the course management system's homepage a statement something like "To get started in the course, watch the video below." So if, as many authors have written, face-to-face teaching is primarily theater, online teaching is—to a large extent—writing, using words to scaffold the structure of an educational experience.

In this environment, word choice matters. For example, while it may be enough, in a face-to-face course, to title the sections of a syllabus "Week 1," "Week 2," and so on, it's better in an asynchronous online-only course to include specific dates (Oct. 9-13, Nov. 6-10) in the titles of modules displayed in a content management system. That way, students accustomed to temporal cues about when to attend face-to-face courses—"If it's 10 a.m. Tuesday, I must be taking the bus to my 'Writing for the Media' class"—at least get a reminder about when to *attend to* an online course. Paradoxically, the course syllabus, though important as a planning and quasi-contractual document in an online course, can become less crucial to students as a reference point about due dates than the course calendar or list of course modules. Woe betide the instructor who inadvertently clicks the wrong assignment due-date box when setting up an online class! That professor may learn that students view online course calendars as inviolable and look at the syllabus once a semester—if at all.

Online, no one can hear you scream: As a result, repetition is important in fully or partly online courses. A professor teaching a fully online course can post a reminder about the content or due date of an assignment in one place but can't guarantee that every student will look at that portion of the course or attend to what is displayed there. Once again, theatrical methods don't work so well online. It's impossible for an instructor using Blackboard or Sakai to stand on a desk or raise his voice to get students' attention while conveying crucial information. So it's necessary to place key information about, say, an assignment due date in multiple places: directly on the instructions for the assignment, in an announcements section of the course and in an email to students. Instructors teaching blended/hybrid courses are wise to make sure that some part of face-to-face meetings addresses key course information students could miss if it were featured only in the online portions of the course.

The power of presence: Some students seem to crave the physical presence of a teacher and classmates and may miss those classroom connections when taking a fully online course. In fact, the first time one of us taught online, students shared both in one-on-one meetings and in teaching evaluations that they hadn't realized they would be "teaching themselves"! Though the course had been meticulously planned, with assignments that built on readings and students divided into small online discussion groups that the instructor closely monitored and contributed to, some students missed the instructor's presence.

Many professors battle perceptions of a lack of presence by, ironically, mirroring in the newer form of online teaching one of the oldest forms of instruction: the lecture. Instructors planning to use lectures in online courses can either make videos of themselves talking directly into the camera or use voice over PowerPoint or Keynote slides, perhaps with a picture-in-picture of the professor in one corner of the slides.

That doesn't mean, however, that online lectures should last for the same amount of time that an in-person course would meet. Students "taking a course" at home or during their commutes likely don't have 60 or 80 minutes to sit, immobile, as they would in a classroom. Instead, online instructors should think about chunking lectures into series of shorter talks of 10 to 15 minutes each. Producing shorter lectures also reduces the chance that a video talk recorded at home will be ruined by a dog barking or a toddler running into the frame!

It should go without saying that a professor's demeanor in a lecture is important if that talk shows his or her face, either as the main video or as a picture-in-a-picture. Clothing—at least on the visible part of the body—should be as professional as one would wear in the classroom. The backdrop of videos, even those recorded at home, should be neutral—a blank wall, a bookshelf, curtains—so that students focus on the message, not the personal, such as a professor's unmade bed. Professors should resist, however, the tendency to want to make every video recording perfect. Coughs happen.

The deal with discussion: Another way to give students a sense of the camaraderie they might form when meeting together in person is to try to replicate classroom discussion online. Most course-management systems have some sort of threaded discussion tool that allows students to respond, asynchronously, to a professor's question or prompt. Small courses can also make use of free third-party applications, such as the business messaging tool Slack. Used wisely and watched carefully by the professor, these discussions can help students develop their knowledge of the course material. A couple of caveats, however, are in order.

First, with most undergraduate groups, merely asking students to "discuss the readings for this week" or "discuss topic X" is not enough.

Instead, professors need to carefully hone a question or prompt that will require students to draw on readings, video lectures or other course materials to provide evidence for a reasoned point of view. The ideal online discussion question is not one that can be answered "yes" or "no" but one that prompts the response "yes, because" or "no, because." Questions that might spark students to answer "maybe, because" and wrestle with some ambiguity are even better.

If the goal of online discussions is to approximate the experience of discussion in a face-to-face course, with its give and take, then instructors need to require more than a single response from each student. Otherwise students may post their thoughts and leave the discussion without reading their classmates' reflections, missing valuable points of view. One way to stimulate discussion is to base some portion of the points available for that course activity on the originality of a student's post—which forces students to read their classmates' writings to avoid duplicating them—and award some points for responses to other students' postings.

In general, online discussions probably work best if they involve relatively small groups of students, say 15 or fewer. If an online course is larger than that, it's probably worthwhile to break the class into two or more groups for the sake of discussions. Ambitious professors can even rearrange these microcommunities mid-semester to foster new intellectual encounters.

Combatting disinformation: A challenge for professors teaching online is battling misperceptions that develop about course content, which can form more easily online than in a face-to-face classroom. Because students are reading and listening to content on their own, without hearing classmates orally ask questions about the material, they may not realize that they have formed a misinterpretation of some information from the instructor or the readings. Professors may not pick up on these misperceptions, as they would in face-to-face courses, until the end of the term, when final papers, projects or discussion-question exams are due. (Many online instructors avoid objective exams because, despite the development of various proctoring technologies, it remains difficult to ensure that students taking objective exams at home aren't using unauthorized aids.)

Sometimes misperceptions about course content come from student misreadings or misunderstandings of course texts or video lectures. Those can be combatted to some extent by having students take open-book, open-readings quizzes periodically throughout the course. Professors may choose to have grades on these quizzes figured into students' course averages or give everyone who completes a quiz the same number of participation points, regardless of score earned. However the points for the quizzes are ultimately recorded, taking the quizzes offers students an avenue for establishing what they know and don't know.

In other cases, misunderstandings develop on course discussion boards when one student makes a factually incorrect assertion, often based on a misreading of course materials—or a failure to read them—and other students repeat that incorrect information. Allowed to go unchallenged, such assertions can lead to students writing final course papers that depend on large factual inaccuracies. It behooves instructors to monitor discussion boards closely, checking in at least once a day and more often near deadline.

When incorrect information is shared, there are several ways to tackle it. The instructor can privately email the student who made the mistake, explaining the error and asking the student to post a follow-up that clarifies the situation. The instructor can also add a carefully worded post to the discussion board explaining the accurate information. Alternatively, the instructor can make and post to the content-management system a short video discussing a more accurate approach to the topic, without naming the student or students who got things wrong.

- RELEVANCE: Post addresses the question asked. 1 point
- SUBSTANCE: Post is thoughtful and substantive and indicates that the poster read the assigned texts. 1 point
- EVIDENCE: Assertions and claims the posts makes are well supported with examples from the readings or videos or relevant outside sources. 1 point
- WRITING: Ideas are clearly expressed and the post is free of grammar errors, spelling errors and punctuation errors. 1 point
- RESPONSES: Student has responded to at least two classmates's posts in a substantive way (not merely saying "I agree" or "I disagree") with respectful language, even if the student has a different viewpoint. 1 point

Sample: Grading Rubric

Online discussions can be a key part of the student experience in an online or hybrid/blended course. They can also be a grading challenge for instructors—so much so that some professors grade only whether students participated or not without focusing on how students participated. Using a rubric like the one shown above, however, can allow instructors to grade discussion posts in a more substantive way relatively quickly.

EXTENDING ANY CLASS INTO THE ONLINE WORLD

Ready-made, free, easy-to-use tools are available for a wide range of purposes: communications from you to students or students to you, show-

FROM THE TRENCHES

Connecting

Sonia Bovio, Arizona State University

For me, one of the most rewarding aspects of teaching is getting to know my students and feeling I've helped them flourish. Satisfaction comes from watching a light bulb go off over a student's head, or fostering a classroom discussion where you learn as much or more from the students as they do from you. Fear of losing that personal connection can inhibit interest in teaching online courses. It's especially intimidating if you are teaching a class of hundreds online, where—as I've discovered—providing individual attention is challenging at best.

Creating an engaging online classroom environment is a process of trial and error. I've learned the following tips from my peers and my own experiences:

1. **Limit interaction on the "little things" so that you spend more time teaching, less time managing.**
   - Have a very clear, detailed syllabus that provides specific information about coursework, assignments, exams and deadlines. Refer to it regularly so students learn to rely on it. If your online learning system allows it, create a syllabus quiz and require it to be completed before unlocking course content.
   - Establish a discussion thread for course-related questions and encourage students to respond to each other. Keep an eye on it, and respond when needed to clarify any confusion, but let it be student-driven. Best practice: Put the syllabus in the thread as a pinned post.
   - If your course requires writing assignments, provide examples of what you expect to receive. This helps prevent misunderstandings on assignment requirements.
   - Send emails or course announcements regularly, and on an established schedule, so students learn to look for them on a certain date and time. Include upcoming deadlines for assignments, quizzes and exams. For example, you could create a Monday morning announcement

telling students what is coming up that week and referring them to specific areas of the syllabus for more details.
- Try to keep online conversations on-topic, but allow students to explore tangents within reason.

2. Position yourself as a trusted advisor.
- Don't let grading be the only time you interact with students in the class.
- Be present in whatever platforms you chose for the class. For instance, if you are using a discussion board, establish a number of posts that you will comment on personally per day, and do so consistently.
- Be open to exploratory questions, and respond in an open-ended way.
- Probe into students' critical thinking by asking questions. In online settings, it's hard to know if a student is "getting it" since you have no visual cues. Regularly query the class and/or individual students to make sure they are engaged.
- For discussion boards with 100+ students, instead of attempting to respond to individual posts, create thread summaries that provide your insights and feedback, and encourage students to respond.
- For smaller online discussion groups (under 100 students), try to respond to each student's posts in a discussion forum at least once throughout the course.
- Make sure your responses are not seen as threatening or condescending, since the opportunity for misinterpretation is heightened online. Every word counts.
- Demonstrate to students that you are enjoying the class by lightening the mood with fun (but relevant) graphics, images and emojis.

3. Be a consistent grader.
- Rubrics are a must!
- While it may not be possible to provide detailed feedback on all assignments if it is a large class, provide at least enough information for students to know what they need to do to improve.
- Set expectations from the start of class that you will not allow exceptions for late assignments or missed exams.

While you'll probably never be able to replicate the intimacy of a classroom online, you can encourage engagement by showing students that you are interested in them as individuals. The larger the class, the more difficult it becomes to provide personal interaction. But, if you define your role up front and set expectations, you should be able to put your energy into teaching, rather than managing.

cases of student work, community forums or instruments for teaching digital literacy and global presence. All are pedagogical tools if regarded as such.

If your school doesn't work with an online management system, you can still get some of the elements normally found in one by setting up a class site with WordPress, something one of us did twice, and relatively painlessly, each semester for nearly 12 years. Within that environment, you can post, create sections, hold discussions and surveys, embed and link to course material and provide showcases for student work. Entire class projects can be created this way, as well, and many—entirely class created—have won awards in AEJMC and other scholastic competitions.

A freestanding course site, with sections that might include a blog, showcases, reading materials, syllabus, assignments, policies, grading criteria, annotated links to resources and more, may need, however, more preparation and maintenance than even someone with development experience wants to give, which is why a switch to a combination of Blackboard, Tumblr and Medium worked as alternative foundation venues. Blackboard covers basics, such as grading, posted material and assignments. We've yet to meet anyone who lauds it as an aesthetically pleasing or easily customizable presentation platform. Nor is it accessible to the outside world; students can't share links to content on the class site via email, Messenger or Twitter. Neither can students (or you) form or join spontaneous or grassroots communities around hashtags or events, or develop professional networks.

Social media, where you can do those things, is a rich pedagogical opportunity. Among oft-overlooked benefits:

- Helps professors learn students' names and faces through frequent reinforcement.
- Helps students know each other; especially helpful with large classes or those drawn from multiple campuses or schools.
- Fast-twitch option for alerting students to breaking news, presumably important in journalism and mass communication courses.
- Utility and ease of access encourages students to develop resource networks beneficial long after coursework ends.
- Promotes professionalism and digital literacy.

It didn't take us long to note that students whose work is displayed publicly tend to invest more care in its preparation. No promises, but experience tends to bear this out—meaning more pride in work for them, and less herding and correcting for the teacher. There's something, too, about allowing a glaring error (so long as it's not libelous or factually wrong or misleading) to remain on view for what could be a global audience. That requires a certain amount of professorial courage and fortitude, though, and there's often a fine line between shaming and propelling a student online while calling out "Fly!"

Needless to say, we hope, shaming's not the point, although having the student experience an "oops" moment and recognize there isn't always a safety net is. Try to always show the student how to fix whatever needs fixing. (**Note:** Documenting the error by taking a screengrab before fixing the online version yourself is another way to go. Share the capture with the student in feedback.) Quick lessons: Spelling counts, headline lengths and sizes matter visually or because of technical limitations, content and presentation need to work together and you never know who's reading (or sharing) your work.

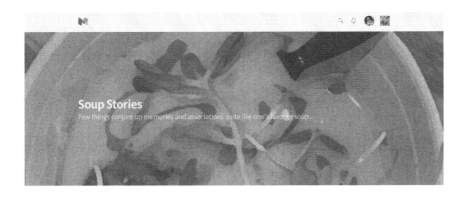

Above are two headers for Medium publications done for advanced online media classes. While there are multiple ways they can be designed, one could, as a class assignment, have students design options and use the best on a rotating basis. These were the results of a class in using Photoshop filters on photos they took themselves.

Rainy Day Spicy Chicken Tortilla Soup

You wake up in the morning and the first thing you do is look outside the window and expect the sun to burst through the glass. But...

Termella Collier
Mar 2

What is Soup

What is soup. What makes a liquid worthy of holding the name soup. Does the liquid have to be hot? Contain some sort of solid? The...

Brianna Stearns
Mar 1

Minestrone Soup on a Thursday

Minestrone soup on a Thursday afternoon. My mom is sitting across from me and my sister is dancing across the street. Every week for the...

Ludwig Ahgren
Feb 26

The Impossibly Rich, Cream of Crab Soup

I'm not entirely sure about residents outside of the states of Maryland and Maine, but in those respective states, cream of crab soup is...

Eddie Poe
Feb 24

Seafood in the Desert: A Love Story

Being what my mom likes to describe as a "poor and starving college student," fancy meals are few and far between and soup, whether made in...

kianna camile Gard...
Feb 24

Food: A Home for the Heart

I love Zuppa Toscana — the ultimate "Italian-style" knock-off soup from the Americanized, yet delicious, Olive Garden. I call Zuppa Toscana...

Brianna Bradley
Feb 23

Soup and I have never had a great relationship.

To say that I hate all soup though would be a lie. You see, there's one soup out there that makes my cold, soup hating heart light up. It...

Lauren Isacksen
Feb 23

The Case Against Soup

Chicken Tortilla Soup

Chowing and Chatting

Shoot First

See it. Shoot it (with a camera). Figure out its story. Write.

Arizona's Painted Sky

Arizona is known for many things, and there is a lot to love in this sunny state.

"Do it for the gram!" balloons

Searching for a suitable subject for this week's assignment, I actually found the perfect idea in my own room.

Erin Vogal-Fox Follow
Sep 2, 2018 · 5 min read

American Story Time

The ebb and flow of audio broadcast entertainment narratives through time

The Blue Mailbox
By Graham Booth

Route and Distraits: Painting of Grover's Mill. Photo Credit: Erin Fox Vogel/ clip Art (Painting)

I can remember it like it was yesterday. My father and I were in the car driving home from his girlfriend's house in Pennsylvania. He told me he had

Medium offers layout (theme) choices to vary the "table of contents" (top left) and story presentations (bottom right). Editing options allow you to send private notes to students, enabling participatory editing and very specific feedback.

Above are four views of one Tumblr site for posting and promoting student work for one class. The "preview," top left, displays almost exactly what shows up online for anyone to see (the content may be centered in the public view, depending on settings). The "archive" view, top right and center, is key to locating stories quickly and can give an excellent overview of a semester's work, month by month. The bottom shows the "dash-board" or work space where each post begins. The formats Tumblr accepts—image, video, etc.—are shown in the icon panel at the top. Tip: If you have students include an assignment hashtag—such as #essay1 or #infographic—you can search on the hashtag and pull up a page containing only those posts. Very handy for grading. Similarly, have students use their last names as tags. A search on a name will then bring up all that student's posts, giving you—and the student—an immediate view as to what has or hasn't been done or has gone astray.

Tumblr and Medium are in their most basic form personal feeds. Students, with a free account, can post multimedia (or unimedia) content that can easily look professional thanks to high design standards and user-friendly tools. But one can set up entire publications as well—similar to a magazine—of student work (see samples, above). Access can be controlled with password protection, search-engine deterrence, or authorization requirements for contributors. When it's time to publish more broadly, the platforms offer promotion and search options, bringing the work to a larger potential audience.

Among other things, while using Tumblr and Medium students learned to:

- Upload work to the university's web server and then create promotion blurbs on Tumblr linking to that uploaded work, or in-text links in Medium.
- Work with HTML to customize posts.
- Follow a publication style so the whole was attractive and consistent.
- Write succinctly and engagingly, and use hashtags in a meaningful way.
- Format photographs and create images appropriate to specific platforms and uses.
- Find and properly use and credit Creative Commons work.

There are multiple resources online for creating content, and they can be used as teaching tools in many ways. The Knight Lab's Timeline JS, for example, is an excellent introduction to using spreadsheets in data-driven multimedia (and it comes with its own tutorial). Other popular software tools include Storify (for curating social media), StoryMaps (for interactive maps accompanying stories), Infogram (for making infographics) and Wix (for building websites). In addition, there are sites that compile resources (such as Journalist's Toolbox and the Poynter Institute), provide in-depth tutorials (UC Berkeley Advanced Media Institute, Lynda.com) or simply serve as global parking places for individually produced tutorials.

A search on YouTube, for example, will bring up a multitude of how-to videos; teachers can use YouTube (or Vimeo, or any other online service) as a repository for an entire course's worth of material (see, for example, the YouTube feed for nancied, ASU faculty associate Nancie Dodge).

FROM THE TRENCHES

How I Learned to Stop Worrying and Love Online Teaching

Dawn Gilpin, Arizona State University

When I was first offered the opportunity to convert my social media class into an online format, I was excited. I'd taken online courses, of varying degrees of effectiveness, and felt I had a solid handle on what worked (and what didn't). I looked forward to tackling the virtual education challenge from the other side of the syllabus. And I could teach in my pajamas if I wanted to! I was #WINNING. Then, I sat down to plan. That's when the panic set in. How could I possibly digitize my teaching style and turn my multilayered class into a fast-moving series of ones and zeroes?

In the three years since, I continued to hone the schedule, assignments, tests and policies. No course is ever completely finished, especially in a subject area as volatile as social media, but I've learned lessons I hope can help others embarking on this virtualization journey for the first time. Many are elements that can enhance any class, but I've found that teaching online amplifies the effects of small details—positive or negative.

1. Be transparent, early and often.

We all strive to be precise in our language, but online classes offer additional barriers to comprehension. Instead of simply asking a clarifying question during or after class, or a quick whispered exchange with someone in the next seat, students need to take the active step of emailing or posting to a dedicated forum if they have questions about course materials or assignments. Reading online encourages skimming, so students may be more likely to miss key details, leading to late work or unnecessary loss of points on assignments. In many programs, online classes are likely to bring in nontraditional student populations unfamiliar with college conventions. They may be anxious about what is expected of them, and feel too shy to contact the instructor directly. This can lead to poor performance not because the students fail to master material, but because of failed communication.

My first semester teaching online, I was surprised to find solidly field-tested assignments were suddenly confusing to a significant subset of students. Odd mistakes and misunderstandings I'd never seen before threw me for a loop. It took me a few tries to fully grasp that a supercharged degree of specificity and repetition were key to overcoming these problems. What felt at first like over-explaining turned out to be just-enough-explaining, especially if I used bullet points and **strategic bolding or highlighting** of key phrases. I learned that providing information in multiple ways meant it was more likely to be absorbed. For example, in addition to an overview of assignments and their associated point values and deadlines in the syllabus, I included the same information in a quick-reference course schedule. I added a breakdown of points in the instruction document, as well as a detailed rubric to explain grading criteria. Content overlapped, but the duplication drastically reduced questions and complaints about grading, and students reported less anxiety about deadlines and scoring.

2. Leave breadcrumbs.

In a physical classroom, the instructor has control over the narrative, from the order in which materials are assigned for reading and viewing, to how discussions are structured. Moving materials into an online course management system means giving up a lot of this control.

Even though I post readings and assignments weekly, preventing students from working ahead (to the consternation of some, but for a specific pedagogical reason I'll explain below), students are free to graze at will from among the week's offerings, which can affect how they interpret and retain content. I was shocked, early on, to find some students took the weekly quiz within minutes after the content became available, when it was obvious they could not even have skimmed the materials. I realized some just want to get work out of the way as quickly as possible, without considering the impact on their learning (or their grade).

I learned to leave strategic breadcrumbs, to help them find their way more easily through the thicket of the week's work while picking up key concepts and skills.

While students won't necessarily read or watch items in the order they are listed in the course management system (CMS), that's a good place to start. If the quiz is at the bottom of the folder after the readings and assignments, that can help. For the readings and lectures themselves, I include both a note at the top of the folder recommending students follow the order, and also a short introductory blurb for each item, explaining why it's included and how it relates to other content. When students understand a certain reading will be easier to understand if they've watched your lecture first, they are more likely to consume the content in the recommended order. It also brings them into the learning process in a way they appreciate.

In many CMS environments, such as Blackboard, you can set conditions for "unlocking" content. For instance, the first week's readings and assignments only become visible to students after they've taken a syllabus quiz and submitted a required academic integrity pledge. I recommend using this feature sparingly, however, since complex chains of access permissions can create headaches for the instructor as well as the students.

Finally, I use mastery quizzes, which students can take as many times as they like right up until the deadline. This type of quiz can include more sophisticated questions that require not just information recall but also syn-thesis of concepts and scenarios that draw upon previous weeks' materials, making them a useful study guide. When the criterion is the last versus the highest score, I've found students are less likely to make random attempts just to get it out of the way, and more likely to review content more than once to earn higher scores and thus improve their learning.

3. Mix it up.

One lesson I learned as an online student is the value of variety. We live in a magical world of technology and information, so we have virtually un-limited options when it comes to presenting that information. In face-to-face classes you can adjust the rhythm and tone on the fly, read the room and switch up your teaching to keep students engaged; online, you have to plan those shifts in advance.

I try to include a range of media, from interactive slideshows to media clips, podcasts to articles from scholarly journals. But variety extends beyond forms of content delivery: including voices from a variety of perspectives, language styles and humor, makes the materials more interesting and appealing, which increases the likelihood students will actually do the reading.

4. Create a community.

The most common positive feedback I receive about my class is that stu-dents enjoy the amount of interaction they have with me and, especially, with their peers. From the weekly discussion boards to sharing and commenting on their work via Twitter, asking and answering questions about assignments, finding links to share with the class, and general chit-chat, I dedicate a lot of time and energy to creating a sense of community among the students. This feeling often persists after the class is over, with former students continuing to follow the course hashtag and sometimes interacting with current students.

My online class is about social media, so all of the activity is pedagogically relevant. I would argue, however, that making students feel connected to the class enhances learning in just about any subject. Social media skills are important in every area of media practice, so it is not hard to justify asking stu-dents to link to and comment on each other's work via Twitter, follow a class hashtag, and find links relevant to the course topics to share with the class.

Building course community can increase your own satisfaction as instruc-tor. If you find it hard to connect with your students online, it can be difficult to maintain your enthusiasm no matter how much you enjoy the subject mat-ter. I've had as many as 300 students in an online class, and one surprising advantage is that I am able to connect directly with more of them than in a face-to-face class of that size, limited by constraints of time and space. Even a frivolous exchange, like swapping silly GIFs on Twitter, may only take a few seconds, but it's fun and helps remind students that you are a real person (and vice-versa).

5. Get personal.

A couple of years ago, I incorporated a new unit into my course to focus on issues of race and gender in social media. These are delicate topics that can be difficult to meaningfully address in any setting, and I worried that the detachment of the online context could lead to heated exchanges and uncivil discourse of a kind rarely seen in a physical classroom. I fretted over my selection of readings, wrote and rewrote my lectures numerous times, and struggled over the wording of discussion questions. The first time the material went live, I nervously refreshed the discussion board page over and over, waiting for the first posts to come through, having no idea what would happen.

What happened—in that instance and every time since—has been surprising, and heartening. My discussion question simply asks students to identify and explain which of the week's readings (or viewings) they found most surprising, and which most resonated with their own experiences, and to explain their answers. The result is an outpouring of feelings and stories. Students share their personal experiences with online bullying and sexual harassment, and their thoughts on race and ethnicity. They comment on their classmates' posts with respect, almost everyone curious and grateful for this opportunity to see the world through the eyes of others. For many students, this is the first time they've directly encountered such a personal perspective vastly different from their own.

While I monitor the discussion closely, I intervene only to correct outright errors such as a fundamental misunderstanding or potential conflict (extremely rare). Mostly, I let the conversation unfold. This frank and open discussion of such sensitive topics is, in my experience, nearly impossible to achieve in a face-to-face setting, especially in a class this size. For a week, we all grapple with the limitations of our own experiences, confront our ignorance and biases, and confess our ignorance without fear of reprisal. This unit is consistently named as one with lasting impact on students, where they learned the most—not just about social media, but about the world and their fellow humans.

After this first eye-opening experience, I immediately went back and rewrote the discussion questions for every week, to directly link the course content to students' own lives. This has further strengthened the sense of community among classmates, which I realized had made it possible to address potentially volatile topics after a few weeks of getting to know each other (we discuss race and gender in the penultimate week of the class, not right off the bat). It also increased interest in even potentially dry topics such as net neutrality and terms of service agreements by making students feel more personally connected to them.

While it's true that an online class can feel like a 24/7 job, and is not for the faint of heart, it also offers exciting challenges and flexibility. If your experience is at all like mine, making the most of this opportunity can make the whole online education adventure deeply rewarding in a way I never imagined before I started out. No apocalypse necessary.

A FINAL NOTE

A theme runs through these takes on online courses and centers on three things: the need for clarity, repetition in multiple ways and places, and accuracy. Important, too, is the need for utility for the professor as well as the students. Is there an easy way to help students understand something? Definitely use it. Is there an easy way to see whether assignments are done, undone or missing? Great.

The loss of control in one way—perhaps the lack of in-person contact—can be mitigated by gaining control elsewhere, particularly by corralling technology to one's own ends. We hope this chapter inspires ways of doing just that.

7

Evaluating the Class

Jennifer Jacobs Henderson
and William G. Christ, Trinity University

You have prepared for your classes; you have written (or been given) a syllabus; you feel good about your ability to show your authentic self; you have figured out a number of exercises or projects you want to require and you know that you will be teaching in person, online or in a mixed classroom.

Now you need to determine how to evaluate your class so that you can tell if it is successful—to know whether your students have learned. Before you determine how to evaluate your class, however, you need to decide why you are evaluating the class: Are you evaluating students to give them a grade ("assessment of learning") or are you evaluating them to help them learn material ("assessment for learning"); or both?

The answer determines how and with which tools you should evaluate your class.

PROGRAMMATIC, CURRICULAR AND COURSE ASSESSMENT

Programmatic Assessment

Even as a first-time instructor, you need to understand that there are different kinds of assessment. All accredited universities in the U.S. are accredited by regional and/or state accreditation bodies with their own guidelines. Journalism and mass communication programs that want to be accredited apply to the Accrediting Council on Education in Journalism and Mass Communications (ACEJMC), which itself is recognized by the Council for Higher Education Accreditation (CHEA). ACEJMC programmatic assessment includes standards dealing with programs defining their mission, governance and administrative structures; describing their curriculum and instruction in terms of course hours and content; fostering diversity and inclusion; using full-time and part-time faculty; engaging in scholarship; committing to student services; providing adequate resources, facilities and equipment; linkages to professional and public service and assessing of student learning outcomes (Accrediting Council on Education in Journalism and Mass Communications 2017a).

Curricular Assessment

Curricular assessment is part of the broader programmatic assessment. Reviewers look favorably on programs (and curricula) where the mission of the program is linked to the university or college mission in which it resides and where the curriculum is linked to the program's mission statement. The goal of curricular evaluation is to determine whether the overall program of study (1) leads to student learning, (2) needs to be modified to reach established goals or benchmarks and (3) contributes to discussions regarding future changes.

Course Assessment

At the course level at which you work, you want to know how your course fits into the curricular goals of your program. Does your course stress skills, knowledge or a mix of both? What is your program's expectations of those students who leave your course? Is there a certain level of understanding or proficiency other faculty expect from the students who take your class? What should students in your class know or be able to do when they leave your class? The things you want students to be able to know or do are typically called student learning outcomes or SLOs.

Teaching or Learning?

The differences between programmatic curricular evaluation and the assessment of SLOs are the *perspective* and *scope* of the view. As Don Grady at Elon University explained: "Be careful not to confuse teaching objectives with student learning outcomes. Teaching objectives reflect the instructional goals of a teacher or program. Student learning outcomes are what is hoped students will gain from a course or a program of study. Obviously, these two concepts are related, but oriented from different perspectives. Assessment is ultimately concerned with what students learn and is focused on the knowledge and skills components of a course, as described by student learning outcomes."

Types of Assessment

There are at least six types of assessment:

1. Diagnostic ("Assesses a student's strengths, weaknesses, knowledge and skills prior to instruction");
2. Norm-referenced ("Compares a student's performance against a national or other 'norm' group");
3. Criterion-referenced ("Measures a student's performance against a goal, specific objective or standard");
4. Formative ("Assesses a student's performance during instruction, and usually occurs regularly throughout the instruction process");
5. Interim/benchmark ("Evaluates student performance at periodic intervals, frequently at the end of a grading period. Can predict student performance on end-of-year summative tests") and
6. Summative ("Measures a student's achievement at the end of instruction") (Teach Thought Staff 2015).

If you grew up in the U.S. public (and most private) systems of education, testing was a "normal" part of your life. There were quizzes, tests, papers, projects within and across classes. There were class, school-system, state-testing and national-testing expectations. Besides tests that suggest which class you should be allowed to attend or tests that compare you to other students in other classes, schools or states, much of our testing in schools over the years has been *interim/benchmark* and *summative* assessment. It is evaluation done at the end of a section or unit in the class or at the end of the class. Many of us give short quizzes or papers during a class (interim assessment), which help students understand what we think is important for the final paper or test (summative assessment). There is, however, a second form of testing called *formative* assessment, which attempts to evaluate a class at a moment in time to help correct problems, reward understanding or assess how a class and the teaching are going.

CLASSROOM ASSESSMENT TECHNIQUES

Classroom Formative Assessments

One of the hallmarks of formative assessment is that it is not for a grade (or the grade counts little). The purpose is not to determine how a particular student is doing, but how the class as a whole is working. CATs, or classroom assessment techniques, provide day-to-day feedback, address student misconceptions about class material or goals and provide useful

Table 7.1. Classroom Assessment Techniques (CATs)

Kind of Evaluation	Name	How It's Done	How to Use	Time Needs
Course knowledge and skills	One-Minute Paper*	During last few minutes of class period, ask students to use a half-sheet of paper and write "Most important thing I learned today and what I understood least."	Review before next class meeting and use to clarify, correct, or elaborate.	Low
	Muddiest Point*	Similar to One-Minute Paper but only ask students to describe what they didn't understand and what they think might help.	Same as One-Minute Paper. If many had the same problem, try another approach.	Low
	Chain Notes*	Pass around a large envelope with a question about the class content. Each student writes a short answer, puts it in the envelope and passes it on.	Sort answers by type of answer. At next class meeting, use to discuss ways of understanding.	Low
	Application Article	During last 15 minutes of class, ask students to write a short news article about how a major point applies to a real-world situation. An alternative is to have students write a short article about how the point applies to their major.	Sort articles and pick several to read at next class, illustrating range of applications, depth of understanding and creativity.	Medium
	Student-Generated Test Questions*	Divide the class into groups and assign each group a topic on which they are each to write a question and answer for the next test. Each student should be assured of getting at least one question right on the test.	Use as many of the questions as possible, combining those that are similar.	Medium

Attitudes, values and self-awareness	Journals	Ask students to keep journals that detail their thoughts about the class. May ask them to be specific, recording only attitudes, values or self-awareness.	Have students turn in the journals several times during the semester so you can chart changes and development.	Medium
Reactions to instruction methods	Exam Evaluations*	Select a test that you use regularly and add a few questions at the end that ask students to evaluate how well the test measures their knowledge or skills.	Make changes to the test that are reasonable. Track student responses over time.	Medium
	Student Rep Group	Ask students to volunteer to meet as a small group with you on a regular basis to discuss how the course is progressing, what they are learning and suggestions for improving the course.	Some issues will be for your information, some to be addressed in class.	High
	Suggestion Box	Put a box near the classroom door and ask students to leave notes about any class issue.	Review and respond at the next class session.	Low to Medium
	Peer Review	Work with a willing colleague, pick a representative class session to be observed and ask the colleague to take notes about his/her impression of the class, your interactions with students and your teaching methods.	Decide method with the colleague. Discussion is best, but a written report may be more useful in the long term.	High

Source: Iowa State University 2017a.
*Some material in this table is adapted from Angelo, T. A., and Cross, K. P. (1993). Classroom Assessment Techniques: A Handbook for College Teachers. 2nd ed. San Francisco: Jossey-Bass Publishers.

information to both the student and the teacher about what is and isn't being communicated (Iowa State University 2017a). They can also help students feel less intimidated in class.

So What Are You Assessing?

CATs have been used to "evaluate knowledge and skills"; "attitudes, values and self-awareness" and "reaction to [the] instruction methods" being used. Table 7.1, with data from Iowa State University (2017b), provides examples of CATs and how they can be used.

Classroom Interim and Summative Assessments

Interim and summative assessment are important parts of evaluating your class (see table 7.2). For example, here is a list of items that can spark your imagination (based on Doyle [2017]). Of course, many items on this list can also be used for formative evaluation if you decide not to grade the assignments:

Table 7.2.   Interim and Summative Assessment

Kind of Evaluation	Pros	Cons
Essay tests	Can get in-depth assessment about all levels of Bloom's taxonomy.	Time to administer in class and time to grade.
Objective, true-false, multiple choice, fill-in-the blank, daily quizzes, pop quizzes, scheduled quizzes and matching tests	Grading can be quick	Tends to stress knowledge more than application, evaluation, and creativity.
Open-book tests, take-home tests, group tests, students make up a test	Most of require use of higher-level cognitive domains. Takes pressure off of class time.	Time to grade. In some courses, memorization might be considered a stepping stone to higher-level concepts.
Individual or group oral presentations (e.g., speeches) with or without visual aids	Emphasizes important element of communication that will be useful in many occupations.	Time consuming in class time.
Webpages or sites	Both the analysis or can open up a whole area of media literacy.	Time consuming if students don't have prior knowledge of analysis or construction.

Kind of Evaluation	Pros	Cons
Written reports, term papers, essays	Can get in-depth assessment about all levels of Bloom's taxonomy.	Time to administer and time to grade.
Role plays; performances; simulations; games, like, College Bowl, Jeopardy; debates, trials; point-counter point, town meetings	Fun, interesting ways of breaking up "normal" routines in class. Students can use their creativity.	Time to administer and need to be clear about how exercises will be evaluated.
Creating videos, DVDs, websites, MPs, magazines, newscasts, commercials	Students can use their creativity. . . stresses the higher cognitive domains like application, synthesis, evaluation, analysis and creativity.	Depending on level of required "professionalism," the projects can take time to teach and grade.
Teach a lesson, case studies, solving problems and problem sets, creating mind maps-content maps, images or drawings	It has been said that you don't know if you really know something until you teach it. Students can use their creativity . . . stresses the higher cognitive domains like application, synthesis, evaluation, analysis and creativity.	How each activity will be evaluated is important. Needs to be linked directly to learning objectives, etc.
Reflective journals, discussion/participation, answer questions from readings, write summary or notes of reading	At best, can see student engagement with material.	Time consuming to evaluate.

ASSESSING STUDENT LEARNING

SLOs are now the currency of most regional and professional accreditation bodies. For a variety of reasons, including cost, outcomes-based education continues to gain traction in the U.S. and elsewhere. In journalism and mass communication education, measuring student learning, based on 12 professional values and competencies, is a critical part of AEJMC accreditation. The ACEJMC values and competencies can be a good place to start if you are unfamiliar with SLOs and how they could be stated (Accrediting Council on Education in Journalism and Mass Communications

FROM THE TRENCHES

Asking Faculty about Classroom Assessment

Many well-regarded professors in communication find assessments can be more than just required activities. They see assessment as providing helpful insights for improving teaching, and even more important, student learning. They also agree that assessment should not be seen as a one-time, all-or-nothing activity. Jennifer Fleming at California State University, Long Beach, recommended viewing assessment "as an ongoing dialogue—a dialogue between yourself and your students as well as between your instruction, student performance and the learning outcomes of your program. As such, you want meaningful dialogue to start as soon as possible, within the first few weeks of the semester preferably. That way you get to know what students know and what they do not know about the course content and adjust your pedagogy (and expectations) before it is too late."

Identifying student learning outcomes prior to selecting assessment tools is essential. Melony A. Shemberger of Murray State University said that "[a]ssessment instruments are plentiful—quizzes, tests, writing exercises and group projects, among others." She noted that it is "OK to use a mix of these, but decide which ones would tell you—and your students—the most about the learning outcomes you want to accomplish." Kim Fox, The American University in Cairo, adds that, "based on the course learning outcomes (LOs)," you should "consider structuring the course by building on the knowledge that they should acquire from each assignment, while also adding challenging elements along the way." According to the "forgetting cure theory" (Hermann Ebbinghaus 1885/1913), Qingjiang (Q. J.) Yao of Lamar University explained, "Students will soon forget much of the new things that they have learned in class if they do not review them quickly and regularly. So beyond the regular reviewing activities in class, the final project is also the final opportunity in the class for the students to review what they have learned and apply that knowledge in generating the project. Those projects' 'learning by doing' approach makes the student retain the knowledge longer with more in-depth understanding" (Anzai and Simon 1979).

One of the important considerations related to assessing student learning is when to begin. Faculty suggest early, mid-, and late-term assessments can all work to accomplish goals. David Tucker of the University of Toledo recommended starting right away. "Try to assess the class early," he stated. "The longer you go without giving them or you some type of feedback will not work to your benefit."

Stacey Irwin of Millersville University suggested a midterm formative assessment. "In the early days of a semester so many things are going on that assessment can play a back seat until midterm," she explains. "I do think a mid-term assessment like Angelo and Cross's (1993) 'Minute Paper' would be really helpful in understanding the concepts students have."

Ultimately, the decision as to whether you select early- or mid-term formative assessments, or a final summative assessment, will be based upon what you need to know and why. Whether it is formative evaluation or summative evaluation, however, it all falls under the concept of assessing student learning.

2017b). Some argue that the 12 competencies and values are too broad to be anything but markers for the further development of specific SLOs. Though this perspective has merit, the standard is clear that all students still need to be able to "demonstrate," "apply" and "understand" very prescriptive requirements.

As you think about what you want students to be able to know and do after taking your class, Bloom's Cognitive Taxonomy (1956) and one of its revisions called the Anderson and Krathwohl's Taxonomy (2001) can be useful (see figure).

Original Domain

- Evaluation
- Synthesis
- Analysis
- Application
- Comprehension
- Knowledge

New Domain

- Create
- Evaluate
- Analyze
- Apply
- Understand
- Remember

Bloom's Original and Modified Taxonomy

The taxonomies are useful because each domain can be evaluated with a different tool. For example, if you think that basic knowledge or remembering facts and ideas are important, then you might want to give multiple choice, fill-in-the-blank, and short-answer quizzes and tests that evaluate memory. If you want comprehension or understanding, then you might need to give short-answer tests or short essays. If your primary concern is to have students use the knowledge (application or applying) then you would need short essays or even projects to get your students to this level. Analysis or analyzing can be done through essays. Synthesis and creating would certainly require a longer form of expression by the student as would evaluation and evaluating. Of course, these levels don't have to be tested via "paper and pencil." They can also be tested orally or through applied, creative media projects.

Sometimes it is helpful to think of student-learning outcomes broadly (e.g., I want students to be able to tell stories using video—synthesis or creating on the taxonomies) and sometimes it helps to be very specific (e.g., I want students to understand and use three-point lighting—comprehension or understanding on the taxonomies.). Whether you articulate SLOs that are broad or specific or a mixture of the two will have an impact on how you evaluate your class.

SPECIAL CHALLENGE: GROUP PROJECTS

Two things you will need to decide before you start your assignment is first, how much you want to evaluate the project process versus the product, and second, how much you want to give grades for individual work and initiative vs. the group as a whole (see Brookhart 2013). The Oxford Centre for Staff and Learning Development suggests seven different ways to assess students in groups:

1. All students get the same mark for group project, e.g., 23 out of 30.
2. All students get separate tasks within a group project, which are assessed separately.
3. All students get the same mark, e.g., 23 out of 30. These are then aggregated, e.g., 69 for a group of three students. They can negotiate individual marks, so long as these add up to 69, i.e., a = 28, b = 19, c = 22.
4. All students get the same mark for the product of the group and then peers assess contributions to process out of an additional 10 marks, e.g., a = 23 + 9, b = 23 + 4, c = 23 + 7.
5. All students get the same mark for original task and then get different marks for an additional task.
6. All get the same group mark for the product, then get individual marks for performance in a group.
7. All get the same mark for the original task, but differentiation is achieved in an exam task based on the group work, where those who worked hard at the first task would be better placed to answer well in the exam (O'Neill 2013).

FROM THE TRENCHES

Faculty Advice on Assessing Group Projects

Group project are always difficult to assess—should you give one grade to the entire group? Individual grades? If so, based on what factors? Marie Hardin of Pennsylvania State University acknowledged the challenges of assigning and assessing group work. "Group projects can be tricky. Generally speaking," she clarified, "I think the instructions and expected outcomes need to be crystal clear—and that students should be able to explain their roles in the project outcome." These complications—and extra time commitment for planning and implementation—may cause new faculty members to avoid assessing group work altogether."

John Turner of Towson University warned against this strategy: "Don't be afraid to assess group projects," he suggested, "especially if the task(s) are relevant to real-life situations in which the students would work as a team (newscast, film, audio production, etc.). This will help make your assessment more 'authentic.'"

Yao at Lamar University agreed, explaining that group projects are important experiential learning opportunities for our students and make especially good summative evaluation tools. "I would recommend assigning a group project as a final assignment whenever it is possible," he said, "simply because group working is such an important skill for almost every field. HR directors surveyed in some research projects kept listing teamwork skills as a priority that they are looking in the new graduates."

Irwin eases her students into group projects by building upon low-stakes collaborative assignments before immersing them in a larger high-stakes project. She explained, "I give students a warmup group project that uses some kind of brainstorming work to help them learn a bit about each other and how to build consensus and share ideas before they are grouped for a larger project with a higher point value."

Many seasoned professors recommend assessing the successes and challenges of a team collectively as well as assessing each student's achievement. Grady at Elon University advised that you should "[f]ind a way to assess individual student work. Some students are skilled in hiding out in a group, and often one or two students are the primary motivating force in a group project. As a result, a single group evaluation (one grade for the group) is not necessarily representative of the collective work of individual students; nor is it representative of specific student learning outcomes. Make sure that each student in a group has a specific responsibility that pertains to one or more of the student learning outcomes of a course. Then report the findings as an aggregated evaluation to reflect all members of the group on all outcomes pertinent to a project."

Many professors recommend including a peer evaluation component in the overall group grade. Glenda Cantrell of the University of Alabama explained:

"In the total project assessment, always include points for peer evaluation (10 points, or a letter grade). After all projects are presented/turned in, give each student a rubric to evaluate their teammates on that scale (i.e., 1-10). Include specific measurements like 'contributed to group discussions' or 'turned in group work on time.'" This way, individuals who don't carry their weight or those who take on more than their share can be identified.

Peer evaluation also helps hold individual members of the group accountable for their contributions. Cantrell suggested including "a section for comments on each teammate. This gives power to the group; it helps *encourage 'slackers' to perform better* and not just allow their teammates to do all the work. It also helps the Type-A personalities feel that they have an outlet if they wind up doing too much of the work."

David Tucker of the University of Toledo agreed that group members need to have a say when determining peer contributions. He suggests that when setting up group projects, you should "[m]ake certain that group members get to either *fire people* in their group or at the very least evaluate them when all is said and done. Most college students hate group projects because they feel that they are the ones who end up doing all the work. Make certain you have a way of identifying the slackers." To determine peer contributions in her course, Fox strongly recommended using continuous feedback through journal entries. "Definitely make it a requirement that they have to submit an *individual journal* when the assignment is complete." She added, "The journal will only be available to the professor/instructor so that the students can openly share their thoughts."

Taking a different approach but still using peer evaluation, Dana L. Chinn of the University of Southern California assigns one grade for the entire group but factors in each student's contribution to the project as a part of the course participation grade. "I give everyone in a group the same grade for the assignment or project," she noted, "but also require that each student complete a peer evaluation form. The form outlines some general criteria (task completion, contribution, teamwork), and requires each student to divide up 100 points among all of the team members, including herself. The student must also explain why she divided the points the way she did. The scores from the peer evaluation forms are factored into the attendance/class participation component of the course grade. I also add my observations about the group dynamics from the in-class group work."

Peer evaluation, although a valuable assessment tool, is often much harder for students to undertake than it initially appears. Making it easier for students to differentiate between strong and weak peers is a must. Dom Caristi of Ball State University said that students "are reluctant to provide good critiques: often they are limited in scope, and way too generous. In fairness, though, grading is the hardest part of my job. To help the *peer evaluation process*, have the students *create the rubric* before you begin the project. Another suggestion is to require that they not only give a score to each student, but also a ranking. A student might give every group member a perfect score for, say, leadership, but it forces them to make judgments if they are told to rank each group member by leadership."

The evaluation criteria for peers and the student need to be identified up front and applied using the appropriate tools. Diana Martinelli of the University of West Virginia said, "It's important to *provide information to students* about performance evaluation scales/processes when groups are first assigned and to require each group member to evaluate not only his or her teammates, but also him-/herself.

Experienced faculty recommend that peer evaluation results not be kept secret but rather shared once completed. "Be sure to share peer evaluations with the students," Caristi exhorted, "[e]ach one should know what was said, but not know by whom."

SPECIAL CHALLENGE: ONLINE EVALUATION

Though courses taught online rather than in person have unique challenges, including the inability to read nonverbal cues and the confusion that can come from texts and emails that have multiple meanings, the assessment of online courses in many ways is the same as assessing real-world courses (see also Prineas and Cini [2011]).

FROM THE TRENCHES

Assessing Online Courses

Many professors agree that good assessment designed for face-to-face courses also makes good assessment online. Marie Harden of Pennsylvania State University said, "I think what makes good assessment off-line makes good assessment online. Make sure the *assessment aligns* with the objectives and course content." Yet, just as with physically present courses, you must "[m] ake a distinction between evaluating what students have learned in an online course, and the assessment of student learning outcomes that support program assessment," said Elon University's Grady. "The extent of material offered in an online course may be considerable and the evaluation of learning using incremental tests and assignments may be highly specific. This is different from procedures that focus on concepts and skills that specifically inform the assessment of student learning outcomes. Online assessment measurement tools may include written works, examinations, presentations and productions." Here, Grady is making an important distinction regarding assessment. The student learning that is being tested is usually specific. The student-learning outcomes of the course that feed into programmatic assessment tend to be much broader.

One of the primary challenges of assessing online coursework is authenticating the student as user. David Tucker of the University of Toledo explained the challenge, stating, "The problem with online classes is you're never quite certain whose work you're assessing." Qingjiang Yao of Lamar University agreed that determining the identity of the person on the other side of the computer is of particular concern. "For online course assessment," he stated, "a key issue is the *test-takers' real identity*: instructors do not know who is really taking the test. . . . Some companies, such as ProctorU," have emerged "to help online course teachers monitor the exams and make sure that the test takers fit the student identity throughout the test," he noted. To address this challenge, Tucker also suggested that professors should "[p]ut *time limits* on exams" and "*give a lot of writing* because that makes it more difficult" to cheat. In addition, Yao said that "[s]tudents are less likely to use substitutes if the course involves *intensive projects or exams*, because the cost is huge. Based on that philosophy, my online course assessments are designed differently."

Taking into consideration the difficulties involved in assessing online courses, experienced professors also suggest different kinds of assignments when designing an online syllabus. "I am always looking for a little *more depth* for online course assignments," said Stacy Irwin of Millersville University, "because I need to be able to gauge if the student is really understanding the assignment. I almost always have a reflective or compare/contrast component so students have to do more than hunt through the ebook for answers."

For strictly online courses, Jennifer Fleming of California State University, Long Beach, explained, "Rubrics are key, especially if one integrates 'discussions.' By discussions, I mean text-based discussion forum exchanges that do not happen in real time. In a way, online discussion forum contributions and responses are mini-essays and therefore should be viewed and assessed as such. This needs to be made clear to students participating in online discussion forum assignments, which can be just as, if not more, valuable than traditional face-to-face discussions because online everyone must contribute to the dialogue, instead of just the handful of students who normally engage in face-to-face discussions."

Rubrics

Once you decide what formative and/or interim/summative assessments you want to use, it might be appropriate for you to use a rubric to aid you in class evaluation. Whether the rubric is explicit and written down, or implicit and in our heads, an argument can be made that we all use rubrics; we all should know what we are looking for when we evaluate our students. Simply stated:

> A *rubric* is a scoring guide: a list or chart that describes the criteria that you and perhaps your colleagues will use to evaluate or grade completed student assignments. At a minimum, a rubric lists the things you're looking for when you evaluate assignments. The list is often accompanied by guidelines for evaluating each of those things. (Suskie 2009, 137-138)

Rubrics can be as simple as a checklist or as complex as a multipart rating scale with multiple learning objectives and extensive descriptions about what constitutes success. Virgil E. Varvel Jr. (2010) identified six common purposes for using rubrics and has provided examples of each: (1) *Formative* assessment occurs during the class, project, or learning process; (2) *Summative assessment* is conducted after a class or program of study has been implemented and completed; (3) *Evaluation*: "In addition to assessing student performance, rubrics can be used to evaluate instructional design and instructional effectiveness"; (4) "*Educative* rubrics are not intended for grading. Instead, they provide guidelines by which students can learn and study"; (5) *Motivational* "rubrics can be used to provide motivation for learners. When rubrics are given out before an assignment is begun . . . students know their expectations and can try to meet them"; (6) *Communicative*: "The one item that can set the communicative rubric apart is when it provides a rationale for final grade" [*emphasis* added]. Rubrics can be used for formative, interim and/or summative evaluation.

When teachers hand out instruction sheets for a project or paper describing expectations, these can be seen as nascent rubrics for formative assessment. Any time instructors give out a final grade with different assignments being given different weightings, they are using a "rubric" for summative assessment. The point is that many of us use implicit or partial rubrics already.

Rubric Types

Rubrics can be categorized as either analytic or holistic. Instructors must consider these questions: Do you want to assess specific components within a performance (analytic) or an overall performance (holistic)? Do you want to assess a general competency (e.g., creative thinking), where the rubric could be used for a number of assignments, or specific components within a task? (See table 7.3.)

Judith A. Arter and Jan Chappuis (2006, 29) suggest you use an analytic rubric "for complex performances or products, especially when you want to use the rubric to help plan instruction or provide descriptive feedback to students, or when you plan to use the rubric instructionally with students (assessment for learning)" while using a holistic rubric "for speed scoring to grade (assessment of learning), to get a general overall look at a

Table 7.3. Types and Uses of Rubrics

Types of Rubrics	Definitions	Focal Uses	Advantages	Disadvantages	Samples
Analytic	Each criterion (dimension, trait) is evaluated separately. Provide specific feedback along several dimensions.	To provide overall evaluation guidelines that clarify how grades relate to performance achievement, such as in course grades.	Gives diagnostic information to teacher. Gives formative feedback to students. Easier to link to instruction than holistic rubrics. Good for formative assessment; adaptable for summative assessment; if you need an overall score for grading, you can combine the scores.	Takes more time to score than holistic rubrics. Takes more time to achieve inter-rater reliability than with holistic rubrics.	Practicum portfolio Rubric/scoring sheet
Holistic	All criteria (dimensions, traits) are evaluated simultaneously. Provide a single score based on an overall impression of achievement on a task.	To break assignments or scores down into separate components for grading (description, analysis, grammar, references, etc.)	Scoring is faster than with analytic rubrics. Requires less time to achieve inter-rater reliability. Good for summative assessment.	Single overall score does not communicate information about what to do to improve. Not good for formative assessment.	Course grading rubric Presentation rubric

	Description of Work	Design	Advantages	Disadvantages	Examples
General	Description of work gives characteristics that apply to a whole family of tasks (e.g., writing, problem solving). Contain criteria that are general across tasks.	Designed to provide general guidance as to expectations, such as for grading of written assignments	Can share with students, explicitly linking assessment and instruction. Reuse same rubrics with several tasks or assignments. Supports learning by helping students see "good work" as bigger than one task. Supports student self-evaluation. Students can help construct general rubrics.	Lower reliability at first than with task-specific rubrics. Requires practice to apply well.	Course grading rubric Position paper Scoring/Feedback Sheet
Task-Specific	Description of work refers to the specific content of a particular task (e.g., gives an answer, specifies a conclusion). Are unique to a task/assignment.	Designed to provide detailed guidance regarding a specific assignment or task.	Teachers sometimes say using these makes scoring "easier." Requires less time to achieve inter-rater reliability.	Cannot share with students (would give away answers). Need to write new rubrics for each task. For open-ended tasks, good answers not listed in rubrics may be evaluated poorly.	Practicum portfolio rubric Research paper Scoring/feedback sheet

Sources: This table is based on work by Susan M. Brookhart (2013), Bonnie B. Mullinix (2017), the TLT (Teaching, Learning, and Technology) Group (n.d.) and the Schreyer Institute for Teaching Excellence (2007).

group, or when the learning target is not complex enough to require more than a single criterion." On the other hand, they recommend the use of a general rubric for "reasoning, performance skill, and product types of learning targets" and a task-specific rubric for "knowledge-level learning targets." (For examples of different kinds of rubrics, see Zimarro [n.d.].)

Rubrics Pros and Cons

There are a number of advantages to using rubrics (c.f., Stevens and Levi 2012). For instructors, rubrics can make grading more systematic, consistent, easier, and faster. In other words, a rubric can systematically lay out the expectations of an assignment and clarify difficult components. Rubrics can help ensure that the same items are being consistently evaluated using the same criteria. Without rubrics, instructors can find they are making the same written comments on many different papers. With rubrics, it is easier to circle what is missing or what needs to be accomplished on a student's project. Rubrics can make grading faster. And, finally, rubrics can "reduce arguments with students" (Suskie 2009, 139) as expectations become more explicit.

Rubrics can also have advantages for students by making a teacher's expectations clear, by showing students how to meet those expectations, by providing timely feedback and by providing templates for students to evaluate their own work. As more and more K-12 teachers develop rubrics, we anticipate that more and more students in higher education will ask for and expect rubrics in our classes. The point is that there are many reasons for using rubrics. They can help both instructors *and* students.

Rubrics can also be helpful for programmatic consistency and assessment. In programs where there are teaching assistants, adjunct professors and/or part-time instructors, rubrics can be one device to help increase consistency among various teachers. When instructors meet to discuss rubrics it becomes an opportunity to clarify learning outcomes, philosophies of teaching/learning and approaches toward grading. If done as an open-ended discussion, the very act of meeting to discuss rubrics can be beneficial. The meeting can lead to the modification and improvement of the rubrics and give faculty new insight into their own pedagogical strengths and weaknesses. Rubrics can also be used to assess the success of a program as a whole. For example, rubrics can be used by outside reviewers to assess a program's senior student portfolios. The results can then be used by a program to see which areas of teaching/learning need improvement.

Of course, rubrics are not free from problems (c.f., Reddy and Andrade 2010; Wilson 2006). They can be too specific or too general; they can be unclear or incomplete; they might give students a false sense that if they "fill in each of the boxes" they should get an "A." Rubrics can also be too complex with too many criteria, and they can be unreliable in their application or not valid in terms of what they are supposed to measure.

If, after thinking about the pros and cons, an instructor or a program has decided to use more explicit rubrics, one of the decisions that will need to be made is which rubric to use.

Evaluating Rubrics

The careful development and creation of rubrics can be hard work. What can be equally difficult is determining if a rubric is performing as intended. Varvel Jr. (2010) recommends monitoring a rubric's validity, reliability, consistency, objectivity and usability. It is common for fine-tuning to take place as a rubric is used.

FROM THE TRENCHES

Advice on Assessment Rubrics

Many talented university professors find rubrics to be an essential element of good assessment. John Turner of Towson University recommends using a rubric, stating that "[a] good rubric benefits both you (the instructor) and the student. For you, it makes grading easier, consistent and fairer and helps the student have a better understanding of what you expect from them on the assignment. The rubric should correlate with the student learning outcome and the assignment to assess it." Melony Shemberger of Murray State University is also a proponent of rubrics for course assessments. "A rubric allows you, the instructor, to plan and assess the instrument more effectively," she explained. "You decide what criteria are important, and how each should be rated or weighted in value. For the student, a rubric gives clarity as to what is expected on a particular assignment or task." Cantrell of University of Alabama strongly agrees. "Rubrics are great!" she wrote, "They help maintain consistency and speed up the grading process."

Martinelli suggests "providing students with the grading rubric when an assignment is made to help them understand what's important and expected. Designing an assessment rubric also forces the instructor to think through the assignment/project/course in advance and to break down its key elements and their emphases, and my advice is to keep them as simple as possible." Like her, Fleming of California State University, Long Beach, "strongly encourage[s] everyone to develop and use rubrics to assess assignments. Rubrics help me think through the goals, directions and mechanics of the assignment as well as more clearly link the assignment with course and program learning outcomes. They also make the grading process more transparent to students. With rubrics, students can literally see how you will approach grading their work. After the assignment is graded, rubrics can serve as conceptual maps documenting and detailing a student's strengths and weaknesses. For example, a student might be strong in research, but weak in essay organization and transitions."

"A rubric is necessary for almost all assignments," added Yao. "It is not only the criteria for the instructor to grade the assignments, avoid grading disputes, but also, or even more importantly, the guidance for students to produce the best projects. I always put rubrics for the major assignments in the syllabi. Rubrics for other projects can be posted on course websites, distributed through handouts, or discussed in class."

Not all faculty use rubrics. "My initial reaction is don't" said Tucker. "The problem with rubrics is the students beat you over the head with them when you get a grade. Essays only marginally work for rubrics. How bad is bad grammar? How can you test whether they approached the problem laid out to a 50 percent maximum?"

Creating Rubrics

Creating a rubric is easy. Creating a useful rubric that has validity, reliability, consistency, objectivity and usability is more difficult. Some argue that students should be involved in the development of rubrics; suggesting that the act of developing a rubric can be educational (c.f., Teachers First 2017). The nonprofit TLT (Teaching, Learning, and Technology) Group (n.d.) suggests six keys steps in the creation of a rubric:

1. Identify the type and purpose of the rubric;
2. Identify distinct criteria to be evaluated;
3. Determine your levels of assessment;
4. Describe each level for each of the criteria, clearly differentiating between them;
5. Involve learners in development and effective use of the rubric;
6. Pretest and retest your rubric.

There are a number of websites that provide templates for the creation and development of rubrics. For example, the "Creating a Rubric: Tutorial" from the University of South Florida's College of Public Health's Educational Assessment and Technology Department (n.d.) walks you through the step-by-step process of creating project rubrics.

Rubistar, which is supported by a grant from the U.S. Department of Education, is a website providing customizable forms where you can create rubrics. The site provides options for rubrics based on the assignment being undertaken, particularly "project-based learning activities." For example, it allows you to create rubrics on common communication assignments such as: "Digital Storytelling," "Web Site Design," "Newscast" and "Persuasive Essay." Several rubric-generation sites were initially designed for K-12 education, but have been modified by university professors. For example, the Multimedia Mania Student Checklist designed by faculty and staff at North Carolina State University for high school students undertaking multimedia projects could easily be modified for use by college students as a checklist before submitting their work (Vasu et al. 2003).

FROM THE TRENCHES

Developing Rubric Criteria

Once you have decided to use a rubric to assess an assignment, project or class discussion, you must then develop criteria that will be used as markers of assessment. Hardin of Pennsylvania State University stated, "The more *specific* the rubric, the better. And there should be nothing on the rubric that hasn't clearly been explicated as a value, competency or skill in the course instruction/content."

Not all rubrics are created equal, though. Grady warns that you also need to "recognize that some *rubrics may not be well suited* for some student learning outcomes. For example, a rubric may work well for assessing knowledge, but not necessarily for the skills used in producing a project. Therefore, rubrics must be developed specifically to assess student learning outcomes for formative assignments and projects, or for summative measures to assess an overall program of study."

Glenda Cantrell of the University of Alabama offers advice on how to begin creating a rubric. "For a good rubric," she said, "write out a list of everything you expect to see in the paper or project. Include basics like correct grammar and spelling, bibliography, etc. Next, determine which elements are most important, which can be combined with another topic, and which elements are least important. Organize these elements in order of importance, then *assign point values* based on their importance. It's easier if these point values are multiples of five. Keep tweaking until you have arrived at a workable number (100 is most common). Plug your elements and point values into Excel and you have a rubric." Diana Martinelli of the University of West Virginia explains that:

an assignment rubric might include some or all of the following: *writing quality* (grammar, punctuation, spelling, consistent/proper style);

research (a minimum quantity of various quality source types); *critical thinking* (evidence of connections and logical conclusions); *creativity* (evidence of original thought/ideas); and *professionalism* (appropriate type size, style, page numbers, adequate margins, title page). I also like to include an *"other"* category on grading rubrics to provide the option of additional bonus points or constructive comments, should students excel and/or falter in ways that the rubric's categories do not adequately capture. When deciding upon the points for each graded element/category, *be careful to weight them* according to the desired key performance areas. *Do the math* to ensure that students can't earn a good grade on an assignment if they don't perform well on its most important elements.

Rubrics need not be created for each assignment—they can also be "borrowed." "Find a rubric that is somewhat standard for the kind of project you are assessing and try that your first semester, and *then tweak it* for future semesters," Irwin recommended. "Or ask a department colleague who teaches the course for an example of a rubric s/he uses. I also highly suggested Angelo and Cross's (1993) *Teaching Goals Inventory* (TGI) to get a clear handle on the top goals you are trying to achieve in your class" (see Iowa State University 2017b).

NOW WHAT?

The main point is DON'T PANIC. When medical students become doctors we say they are now "practicing." The same could be said about university professors. We continue to learn as teachers throughout the course of our careers. Hopefully, this book will give you the knowledge to become a proficient teacher. However, becoming a great instructor is a matter of trial and error, give and take and a willingness to make mistakes and move forward. Our best students are the ones who will challenge us and keep asking, "Why?" As we develop our philosophy of student and class evaluation, we need to be able to answer those questions: "Why are we using a specific test or requiring a paper topic?" "Why are we evaluating them in the first place?"

REFERENCES

Accrediting Council on Education in Journalism and Mass Communications (2017a). "Nine Accrediting Standards." http://www.acejmc.org/policies-process/nine-standards/.

Accrediting Council on Education in Journalism and Mass Communications (2017b). "A Guide to Assessment of Learning Outcomes for ACEJMC Accreditation." http://www.acejmc.org/resources/acejmc-guide-to-assessment/.

Anderson, L. W., and Krathwohl, D. R. (2001). A taxonomy for learning, teaching, and assessing: A revision of Bloom's taxonomy of educational objectives. New York: Longman.

Angelo, Thomas A., and Patricia K. Cross (1993). Classroom Assessment Techniques: A Handbook for College Teachers. 2nd edition. San Francisco, CA: Jossey-Bass, Inc.

Anzai, Yuichiro, and Herbert A. Simon (1979). "A Theory of Learning by Doing." Psychological Review 86 (2): 124-140. Doi: 10.1037/0033-295X.86.2.124.

Arter, Judith A., and Jan Chappuis (2006). Creating and Recognizing Quality Rubrics. Upper Saddle River, NJ: Educational Testing Service.

Bloom, B. S. (ed.). (1956). Taxonomy of Educational Objectives. Vol. 1: Cognitive Domain. New York: McKay.

Brookhart, Susan M. (2013). Grading and Group Work: How Do I Assess Individual Learning When Students Work Together? Alexandra, VA: ASCD Arias.

———. (2014). "How to Create and Use Rubrics for Formative Assessment and Grading." http://www.ascd.org/publications/books/112001/chapters/What-Are-Rubrics-and-Why-Are-They-Important%C2%A2.aspx.

Brookhart, Susan M., and Anthony J. Nitko (2008). Assessment and Grading in Classrooms. Upper Saddle River, NJ: Pearson Education.

Doyle, Terry (2017). "Fifty Ways to Assess Learning." https://learnercentered teaching.wordpress.com/teaching-resources/fifty-ways-to-assess-learning/.

Ebbinghaus, Hermann (1885/1913). Memory: A Contribution to Experimental Psychology. Trans. H. A. Ruger and C. E. Bussenius. New York: Teacher's College, Columbia University. http://psychclassics.yorku.ca/Ebbinghaus/index.htm.

Frantz, David W. (2004). "Leaderless Groups." In G. R. Goethals, G. J. Sorenson and J. M. Burns, eds., Encyclopedia of Leadership. Thousand Oaks, CA: Sage Reference. Doi: http://dx.doi.org/10.4135/9781412952392.

Iowa State University (2017a). "Classroom Assessment Techniques: Quick Strategies to Check Student Learning in Class." http://www.celt.iastate.edu/teaching/assessment-and-evaluation/classroom-assessment-techniques-quick-strategies-to-check-student-learning-in-class.

Iowa State University (2017b). "Teaching Goals Inventory." http://fm.iowa.uiowa.edu/fmi/xsl/tgi/data_entry.xsl?-db=tgi_data&-lay=layout01&-view.

Mullinix, Bonnie B. (2017). "Rubrics." http://webpages.charter.net/bbmullinix/rubrics.htm.

O'Neill, Geraldine (2013, October 10). "Assessment: Assessing Group Work (Including Online)." https://www.ucd.ie/t4cms/UCDTLE0065.pdf.

Prineas, Matthew, and Marie Cini (2011, October). "Assessing Learning in Online Education: The Role of Technology in Improving Student Outcomes" (NILOA Occasional Paper No.12). Urbana, IL: University for Illinois and Indiana University, National Institute for Learning Outcomes Assessment. http://www.learningoutcomeassessment.org/documents/OnlineEd1.pdf.

Reddy, Y. Malini, and Heidi Andrade (2010). "A Review of Rubric Use in Higher Education." Assessment and Evaluation in Higher Education 35 (4): 435-448.

Rubistar (n.d.). "Create Rubrics for your Project-Based Learning Activities." http://rubistar.4teachers.org/index.php?screen=NewRubric&sectionid=3#03.

The Schreyer Institute for Teaching Excellence (2007). "The Basics of Rubrics." http://www.schreyerinstitute.psu.edu/pdf/RubricBasics.pdf.

Stevens, Dannelle D., and Antonia J. Levi (2012). Introduction to Rubrics (An Assessment Tool to Save Grading Time, Convey Effective Feedback, and Promote Student Learning. Sterling, VA: Stylus Publishing, LLC.

Suskie, Linda (2009). Assessing Student Learning: A Common Sense Guide. 2nd edition. San Francisco, CA: Jossey-Bass (John Wiley & Sons).

Teach Thought Staff (2015). "6 Types of Assessment of Learning." http://www.teachthought.com/pedagogy/assessment/6-types-assessment-learning.

Teachers First (2017). "Rubrics to the Rescue." http://www.teachersfirst.com/lessons/rubrics/involving-students.cfm.

The TLT (Teaching, Learning, and Technology) Group. (n.d.). "Rubrics." http://www.tltgroup.org/resources/rubrics.htm.

University of South Florida, College of Public Health, Educational Assessment Department (n.d.). "Creating a Rubric: Tutorial." Modified February 27, 2017. http://health.usf.edu/publichealth/eta/Rubric_Tutorial.

Varvel, Jr., Virgil E. (2010). "Pointer and Clicker Article: Rubrics." http://www.ion.uillinois.edu/resources/pointersclickers/2004_03/creating.asp.

Vasu, Ellen S., Jane Steelman, Judy Lambert and Elizabeth Bean (2003). Multimedia Mania Student Checklist. Revisions by: North Carolina State University Multimedia Mania Team. Original Rubric Developed for ISTE's HyperSIG by: McCullen, Caroline, Jamie McKenzie and Terrie Gray. https://www.ncsu.edu/midlink/mm2002_rubric.kids.pdf.

Wilson, Maja (2006). Rethinking Rubrics in Writing Assessment. Portsmouth, NH: Heinemann.

Zimarro, Dawn M. (n.d.). "Creating a Rubric for Evaluating Media Projects." http://marymac.pbworks.com/w/file/fetch/45285274/utexas%20creatingrubrics%20for%20media%20projects.pdf.

8

Preparing for Next Semester

Carol B. Schwalbe, University of Arizona

The semester has come to its usual frenetic end. You breathe a sigh of relief and promise yourself that you'll begin preparing for next semester as soon as the student evaluations arrive or after you finish that research paper. But then the weeks speed by. Before you know it, classes are about to begin, and you're scrambling to revise your syllabus and prepare for next semester.

The tips in this chapter will help you tweak your syllabus as the semester rolls along. They will also suggest ways to improve your courses by eliminating bad habits or mannerisms and by incorporating feedback from student evaluations, other instructors, senior faculty and mentors.

ASSESSING TEACHING EVALUATIONS TO IMPROVE

Whether student ratings make you smile, grimace or gnash your teeth, evaluations of your teaching effectiveness do matter. They drive decisions on hiring, promotion, tenure and raises. Mounting evidence, however, questions their validity. Researchers have observed that females, professors of color and instructors with accents tend to receive lower scores. So do instructors who teach large lecture classes.

These issues notwithstanding, what can you do to deal successfully with the scrutiny and learn from the feedback?

Natalie Tindall, chair of the Department of Communication at Lamar University, offers the following tips:

Find a time and place where you can digest the evaluations without interruptions.

Pay attention to the comments. They may help you determine what to do or change for next semester. Search for common themes, such as unfair testing / assignments / grading, classroom policies or unclear expectations. If you see clumps of these emerge in the student feedback, a change in approach might be necessary.

Know that you aren't alone if you receive bad feedback. Every professor does not receive glowing comments from every student.

Consider the context of the semester. Think about what else was happening in your professional and personal life. Are you starting a new job on a new campus? Is this your first time teaching the course? Is this your first time teaching? Analyze your own experiences and determine if these may have had an influence on the class.

Separate personal attacks from honest concerns about the course content. I once had a teaching evaluation that claimed my "feet were too big" for my body. Thanks, anonymous student, but I can't do much about genetics. That feedback was not useful at all, but it was one personal attack buried in a plethora of thoughtful, nuanced comments from students who wanted the class to be better. Comments about the order and flow of the class may sting and feel personal, but they are not. Things such as vague in-class communication and disorganized course content can be adjusted for the next semester. Shoe size, alas, cannot be changed. (Note: If you receive any racist, sexist, abusive or threatening student feedback, report those comments to the appropriate university officials.)

Take control of the evaluation process. Do not wait until the end of the year to hear what your students think. Gather this information at key semester points. Next semester, try one or all of the following:

- **Explain the purpose and importance of evaluations.**

- **Ask your students about their teaching pet peeves.** Pass out index cards on the first day of classes, and ask each student to write down any complaints regarding teaching behaviors. This insight might help you modify the class, your delivery style or homework assignments.
- **Build ongoing evaluations into the class structure to check the pulse of the class.** These evaluations can be informal minute papers, where students capture the one "big idea" from the lecture and address any questions they have, or a "muddy points" exercise, where students write (without names) what topics in the lecture or discussion were not clear.

- **Adopt a holistic approach to the evaluation of your teaching.** The numbers on student evaluations tell just one part of the story. You can always broaden your teaching portfolio to include syllabi, assignments, exams and examples of student work. You could even track students' progress once they leave your class.
- **Ask a trusted colleague to observe your class and provide constructive feedback.**
- **Understand the teaching expectations for your department and university.** Did you fall below or land above those numbers?
- **Use your school's teaching and learning center resources.**
- **Read or re-read teaching guides,** such as Wilbert J. McKeachie's "Teaching Tips." Even if you have teaching experience or read these books years ago, you still might find a valuable nugget.

CONTINUOUSLY TWEAKING YOUR SYLLABUS

You can retool your syllabus as soon as the semester begins. Lee Hood, who teaches broadcast news at Loyola University Chicago, keeps an extra copy of the syllabus and uses Microsoft Word's track changes to mark things she wants to tweak the next semester. "I find this particularly important for classes I'm teaching for the first or second time," she said, "as well as for the spring semester, when it's a longer break before I'll be putting the next syllabus together."

As the semester progresses, Sally Ann Cruikshank jots down notes every time she finishes a class activity or grades an assignment. What did everyone get right? Were there things that everyone struggled with or missed? Cruikshank, who teaches digital journalism at Middle Tennessee State University, looks at the notes again while preparing her syllabus for the next semester. By then, her notes have had time to "marinate."

Toward the end of the semester, you can ask students which assignments they liked and which ones they didn't—and why. Maddie Liseblad, who teaches editing at Arizona State University, said students will speak up if they view your classroom as open and safe. "It's usually a very lively discussion, and I think it makes them feel empowered in a way," Liseblad said. "This discussion helps me gauge if I should do more of one type of assignment and perhaps drop assignments. While I generally get some of this type of feedback on the course evaluation, having a dialogue with the students is incredibly beneficial because I can then dig deeper into what exactly it is they liked or didn't like. It also helps me get a better feel for how these students learn. I'm much older than my students, so understanding what makes them excited and what's helpful makes me a more effective instructor."

As you collect material for the following semester, keep it organized. Bill Silcock, an assistant dean at Arizona State University, emails himself articles, tweets and Facebook posts for future classes, then stashes them in a folder on his desktop. He stores infographics and other visual material on Pinterest, which he can link to from his syllabus. Other organizational tools include free cross-platform apps such as Evermore, which lets you take notes, then organize, archive and store them on any device for easy retrieval.

FROM THE TRENCHES

Strategies for Revising Syllabi

Mindy McAdams, University of Florida

With a focus on digital journalism and technologies for storytelling, I have to revise every syllabus every year. My strategy is different for different courses.

For a more theoretical graduate course about communication and a democratic society, I usually replace about 15 to 20 percent of the readings, even if I keep the same topics as last year. Throughout the year I download and save PDFs from journals in a folder marked for that course. I don't always read them before I save them. I use emailed tables of contents from all the major journals to keep up. In August I sort through those articles and choose those that address newer ideas. If they suggest a new topic, I retire and replace an existing topic.

For the journalism coding courses I teach, I have to keep up with changes in best practices for web development. I do that largely via Twitter, by following journalists and news outlets that blaze new trails for story formats and presentation. Usually I bookmark examples and tutorials using Pinboard (https://pinboard.in/about), tagging them appropriately so I can find them later. I also depend a lot on what professionals present at the annual conferences of the Online News Association (ONA) and the National Institute for Computer-Assisted Reporting (NICAR). Based on those sources, I change materials or assignments as needed, although not usually in the middle of a course!

I use a textbook in only one course (Introduction to Web Apps), so I have to find and update all the assigned readings.

I use a separate WordPress.com site as a syllabus for each of my courses, so it's easy to link to online sources, and it's also easy to update via the WordPress dashboard. I try to keep the "course schedule" page streamlined so it's mostly links, with a heading for each week in the semester. You can see all my syllabuses here: https://github.com/macloo/course-syllabi.

For the graduate course, I post assignment instructions weekly on the WordPress site. For my skills courses, which have more detailed assignments, I use Google Docs because they are so easy to format and revise. Students submit their assignments in our course management system, but instructions are provided via a link to the Google Doc. This also simplifies managing the assignment documents because they are organized in my Google Drive, with separate folders for each course.

WATCHING OTHER TEACHERS

Observing other instructors can be inspiring and a great source of new strategies for conveying information and engaging students. "When you've been teaching the same thing over and over for a long time, it's easy to get stuck in doing things the same way, especially if those methods have proven to be effective," said Lani Diane Rich at Syracuse University. "By incorporating methods you see other professors using, you can keep things fresh, not just for the students but for yourself. When you're energized and excited, the students get energized and excited."

Observing master teachers can also be intimidating, particularly if you're not the type of instructor who cracks jokes or wears funny hats to class. Be yourself. Often, the most influential teachers are those who care about their students or inspire them—with or without the wisecracks or the grouchy cat hat.

To get the most from observing other teachers, attend as many classes as possible, said Carol Holstead, who teaches writing, design and public speaking at the University of Kansas. Early in her teaching career, Holstead observed a design professor's studio class for an entire semester. "That experience changed the way I taught my own classes," she said. "I had a tendency when giving feedback to tell students what they should do. My colleague excelled at leading students to their own solutions by asking them pointed questions about why they made the decisions they did on their projects. Of course, students wanted him to tell them what to do, but while that might be most expedient, it doesn't teach students to think critically and solve their own problems."

Team teaching is another way to immerse yourself in observation (as well as receive mentoring). Holstead has team-taught several journalism courses. "Each time, it has made me more aware of my own strengths and weaknesses," she said. "It can be uncomfortable to teach in front of colleagues—it's human nature to feel inadequate—but invariably you will learn through comparison, and, if you team-teach with an experienced colleague, you also should ask for feedback. In a team teaching situation, a colleague may not want to volunteer it."

FROM THE TRENCHES

Adapting Presentation Techniques for Flopsy Bops

Ted Spiker, University of Florida

I love to watch others teach or present—and not just in the regular classroom setting, but in any area of performance or presentation. That's why I think it's useful to look at actors, comedians and anybody else who works a room—not just teachers. Most of the time when I'm looking at others teach, I notice things like pace between lecture and interaction and how well they hold a room as they weave between information, stories and whatever form of interaction they choose for their class or audience.

One of my favorite things to do is look for small techniques in delivery and performance. The most engaging people, of course, are the ones who really use rhythm and variety in their voice to create drama, humor and interest around the content. So while the content has to be there for our classes, of course, the delivery does too.

On a study abroad trip in London, one of our tour guides was one of the most engaging presenters I have ever heard. She used unpredictable language that she knew would be fun for her audience—like "flopsy bops" for the students on the trip and "popped her clogs" to say someone had died. But she was even better at her voice fluctuations—changing the pace and speed of her sentences, dramatically shifting between a regular tone and then going very deep and low to emphasize a word or syllable.

Now, not everyone can pull it off, because the presentation has to match the personality. It can't be over-scripted, or else it comes off as contrived and unauthentic, but it gave me a lot to think about in terms of using a wide range of voice/tone techniques to really experiment with delivery. So this fall, I'm going to experiment more with tone, pace, volume and creative language, though I won't probably won't call the class a room full of flopsy bops.

FROM THE TRENCHES

Be a Student

Carol Zuegner, Creighton University

The best teaching advice I can offer professors is to be a student.

When I became department chair, I sat in on all the professors' classes to help evaluate their teaching. While the time spent afterward talking with each professor was instructive, the true winner in this exercise was me. Sitting in on a variety of classes across disciplines (our department combines journalism, graphic design and computer science) gave me insights into my own teaching and ways I could improve it or just different ways to think about the material.

I was fascinated by the critique I observed in the data visualization class. Each student took a turn to be evaluated and then to document the evaluation of another student—writing down the comments and offering a deeper commentary of her own. What a great idea for presentations in my social media class.

Another professor banned the use of cellphones in class but gave students a two-minute digital break just as attention was flagging in the 75-minute class. It was a nice break and something to consider for my classes.

A computer science professor developed an in-class system to evaluate student learning along the way—a quick question about material that had just been covered. Perhaps I could figure out a way to do a similar exercise in my own classes. Helping students sift through a lot of material and highlight what's important reminded me of the popular pub quizzes that keep students engaged.

Experiencing a class as a student offered a few revelations and reinforced my own ideas. A 75-minute class is long. Too many words on a PowerPoint slide are deadly. Finding the balance between just enough time to cover a topic versus spending too little/too much time is tricky. Handwriting on a whiteboard can be hard to read from the back of the room.

Good professors find their own voice and style, but continued good teaching also takes work and the willingness to try something new.

PEER OBSERVATION

When a senior faculty member comes to your classroom to observe your teaching, don't panic. The mutual goal should be to improve your teaching. Both you and the observer should benefit from this process.

Often, professors receive peer evaluations only when they go up for promotions and tenure, "then for the next 30 years, who knows if we're still any good at teaching?" said Silcock at Arizona State. "I believe quality journalism schools focus on teaching."

Peer observations should not be a surprise drop-in visit. "No faculty member, whether brand new or a senior scholar, should be surprised by having a colleague pop in and watch a class," Silcock said. "Let's face it. Some days, we just aren't on our A game."

You and the observer should meet at least a week ahead of time to agree on a date and class for the observation, discuss your plan for that class, decide whether the observer should sit, and set up a time to meet a week or so later. The observer should also ask for a copy of your syllabus.

See the Classroom Observation Checklist at the end of the chapter for items typically included in an observation.

Peer evaluations might not provide as much valuable feedback as you would like. Sometimes, evaluators want to be polite and positive, or perhaps no one else at your school teaches the same subject as you do. In that case, said Cruikshank of Middle Tennessee, chat with people who teach in your field at conferences or in casual conversation. She has picked up some great ideas about class activities, assignments and lectures this way.

FROM THE TRENCHES

Observing and Assessing Other Instructors

Sharon Bloyd-Peshkin, Columbia College Chicago

One of my administrative duties is course supervision, which includes observing faculty members and then sharing those observations with them and the college administration as part of their periodic evaluations.

I know that faculty members—full time and part time—are nervous about this process, so the first thing I do is reassure them about my motivations: I am there to help. Everyone, I say, benefits from having someone else observe their teaching, and everyone has areas in which they can improve, including me. I often tell them about Atul Gawande's 2011 story in The New Yorker, "Personal Best: Top Athletes and Singers Have Coaches. Should You?" Gawande realizes his performance as a surgeon has plateaued, so he invites a renowned retired surgeon, Robert Osteen, to observe him performing an operation and provide some tips. Gawande was arguably at the top of his game, but Osteen's observations helped him improve.

I also make sure everyone knows what my role is in the class. I tell the faculty member to feel free to ask me questions or call on me. I tell the students I'm there because all faculty are periodically observed. This ensures they don't think their instructor has done anything wrong, and it demonstrates that the department and the school take the quality of teaching seriously.

During the class I take prolific notes. I pay special attention to the following things:

- How much of the time is the instructor's voice heard?
- How much of the interaction is instructor/student and how much is student/student?
- Do all the students have opportunities to talk or contribute in other ways?
- Does the instructor move around the room or remain at the front?
- Does the instructor write key takeaway points on a board or equivalent (a form of note-taking prompt)?

- Does the instructor help students discover what they are supposed to be learning (instead of telling them)?
- How does the instructor handle "incorrect" answers?
- When students are asked to critique something, do they know what the standards are?

This is not a one-size-fits-all list of best practices. It's also not a complete list. But it is a way to figure out why students are or are not engaged. If a teacher talks too much, if all communication is between the teacher and one student and not between students, if the room is physically static and the knowledge flows only from teacher to students, that helps explain why students aren't engaged and probably aren't learning as much.

What I'm looking for is a classroom in which students actively and productively engage with each other in the process of learning. This can look very different, depending on the personality and style of different teachers, but be equally successful.

After the observation, I meet with the instructors to talk about how they felt the class went and to see if there's anything else they think I should know about the class. Then I write up my observations, prefacing them with any extenuating circumstances the instructor told me about.

The first person who reads my observations is the instructor. I welcome a discussion of my observations before I finish filling out the required evaluation materials, and we talk about ways to address any weaknesses I noted. Here I think about my favorite physical therapist, who never prescribes more than three exercises between sessions. "If I give you three, you'll do all of them," she said. "If I give you ten, you won't do any of them."

Finally, I submit the observations and evaluation document to the college. My goal is to ensure that instructors continue to regard me as a resource.

USING MENTORS TO GET HELP

Mentors matter. They can provide career advice, inspiration, support and a friendly ear. Research mentors can co-author papers with you, comment on your articles and suggest journals where you can submit your work. Teaching mentors can give you syllabi, share course materials and recommend ways to sharpen your classroom performance. You can discuss your concerns with trusted mentors and ask for their insight.

Your department may have a mentoring program, but you should also ask colleagues who are good teachers to mentor you. New faculty, however, are often reluctant to ask for help with their syllabus or classes. "I'm not territorial about my classes, and I will gladly share an entire course," said Holstead at Kansas. "People should ask for help, and experienced teachers should pay attention and step up when they can see that someone needs the help."

You can also develop mentors outside your university. Seek their advice about teaching and research at conferences or other get-togethers. They might be willing to write letters of support for promotion and tenure.

FROM THE TRENCHES

Mentoring for Successful Teaching

Carol Holstead, University of Kansas

A colleague was struggling with teaching a required entry-level journalism research and writing class. He was in his second year at Kansas and had taught only upper-level courses. He had worked professionally for the Associated Press, so he had a strong background in journalism. However, that experience also made it hard for him to teach students who had never written a news story or a news release. His feedback tended to be heavy handed and demoralizing. His intentions were good, but he had yet to learn how to teach beginners. He knew my students did better work with less feedback from me.

During his first semester teaching the course, I volunteered a lot of advice. His second semester, he asked me to take a more hands-on approach to mentoring him. I gave him my syllabus, assignments and stories I had graded so he could see the nature and tone of my comments. I advised him to assign fewer stories and allow students to rewrite every major assignment. I suggested that he do individual coaching on students' final project (there is no substitute for an editing appointment). We talked often. I offered feedback on his grading. I counseled him on tone.

He followed my advice and had a revelatory experience about his teaching, but he would not have had that breakthrough had he not willingly submitted himself to my feedback. I mentored him as I did my own students—I was clear and supportive. Good teachers want to mentor inexperienced teachers so they will become better, and you should seek out their advice.

FROM THE TRENCHES

Developing a Productive, Satisfying Mentor Relationship

Susan E. Swanberg, University of Arizona

Before entering a mentoring relationship, both parties should understand what the relationship is—and is not. First, mentoring is not the same as management. A mentor doesn't report to the manager about the mentee, nor does the mentor contribute to performance reviews. To do so undermines the mentee's confidence in discussing difficult issues with the mentor.

Second, mentoring relationships can be formal or informal. A formal relationship is a structured teaching, counseling or advising relationship initiated by an organization, while an informal relationship is a looser relationship between two individuals.

Third, the parties should decide whether the relationship will be mentor centered, mentee centered or a relationship that benefits both parties. A mentee-centered relationship helps the mentee meet career and other goals. A mentor-centered relationship helps the mentor gain management experience. The two types of relationships are not mutually exclusive, but the goals should be transparent to both parties.

Fourth, will the mentor be an adviser or an advocate who takes a stand regarding the mentee's issues? Failing to discuss these roles can leave the mentee feeling abandoned when a difficult issue arises.

Once the relationship is defined, the parties should set up lines of communication, decide on goals, and, if desired, schedule meetings to help sustain the relationship.

Keep these tips below in mind to create a successful mentoring relationship:

1. Define the responsibilities of the mentor and mentee and the expected outcomes.
2. Decide what areas the mentee needs help with, such as how to adjust to the institutional culture or achieve career goals. Sometimes the mentee does not know what issues are important, in which case the mentor can suggest topics. The mentor should ask—repeatedly and not judgmentally—whether the mentee has areas of concern to discuss.
3. Decide whether meetings will be helpful. Will they be scheduled or held only if issues arise? If there will be meetings, how often will the parties meet and what are the expected outcomes?
4. Decide how long the relationship will last. Is there an institutional limit on the length of the mentorship? Will there be a milestone, such as promotion or tenure, that signals the end of the relationship?

ELIMINATING BAD HABITS OR MANNERISMS

Encourage students to challenge your bad habits, usage and mannerisms. "I think remaining humble and open to correction sets the standard for the students," said Ian Punnett, who has taught at Ohio Northern University and recently obtained his PhD from Arizona State University. "It keeps them from feeling like I am trying to hit their 'shame' buttons."

Favoritism—or the perception of favoritism—can cause trouble. Teachers are human, so you'll likely be drawn to certain students. It's normal to feel a kinship with them. Their classmates, however, might resent the extra attention you give them. Do you always praise the "best" students or showcase their work? Do other students feel left out? Whether in your interpersonal relations or classroom demeanor, try to be as fair as possible. Encourage all students. Make the same offers of extra assistance available to everyone.

Maybe you show favoritism by always calling on the same students. To avoid this tendency, Silcock at Arizona State relies on a seating chart in large classes. After the students pick their seats, they're locked down for the rest of the semester. That way, he can learn the students' names and avoid calling on the same ones all the time.

Consider how you respond when you ask your class a question. When hands shoot up, do you immediately call on volunteers? If so, many of the other students won't even bother to think about the answer. They have come to learn that eventually someone else will give the answer.

Or, if there's radio silence for two or three seconds, do you jump in with the answer? Many instructors struggle with engaging everyone in dynamic classroom discussions because they don't give students enough time to answer the question or address the issue at hand. One thing that might help you become comfortable with uncomfortable silence is an old journalist's trick. "When I ask a question, I just wait until someone finally answers it," said Cruikshank of Middle Tennessee. "This way, students start talking to avoid the awkward silence. Usually, I only have to do this once!"

When instructional designer Kelly L. Jones asks a question and no one responds, she waits a full minute, sometimes up to two minutes, to give students the time and space to craft their answer. "If there still is no response, I will call on a student," she said. "But the students are allowed to pass the question to one of their classmates or ask for a volunteer to help them answer the question."

When you call on students, palm, don't point. Jones said this technique makes a positive difference when facilitating a group discussion. "Instead of pointing at students to call on them, I now extend my arm toward them with my palm up. The 'palm up' hand gesture offers a more inviting, respectful invitation to participate than pointing."

Mix it up. Avoid predictability that students might perceive as unfairness. When you pass out papers, for example, don't always start at the front of the room. When students work together, vary the pairs and small groups. Otherwise, the same students tend to keep working together.

You can also avoid predictability by working the room. "Move around," said Ken Fischer, who teaches broadcast production and journalism at the University of Oklahoma. "Don't stay stuck to the front. Of course, logistics like technology sometimes make this difficult."

If you're teaching a seminar and prefer to sit at a table, move from seat to seat over the course of the semester instead of always plunking yourself at the front of the room.

Avoid telling too many war stories. "Blend in personal experiences as you explain material and keep it short," Fischer said. "Students usually tire of war stories unless, of course, the instructor was the late Walter Cronkite or is former LA Dodgers announcer Vin Scully."

Fischer also cautions against too many guest speakers. Exposure to guests is important, but one or two a semester is plenty for a skills course.

Create a positive environment. Perhaps more important than the best-written syllabus or the most creative lesson plan is the emotional environment that the teacher creates in the classroom. Neuroscientists have observed that when people listen to a lecture, their brains synchronize with the speaker's brain. As teachers, "We invite students inside our brains," said Miglena Sternadori, who teaches journalism and mass communication at Texas Tech University.

"The most important element of teaching is internal, not external," Sternadori said. "If we are bored, angry, depressed, all these emotions are likely to be present in the tone of our speech and transfer onto the students. A teacher can be organized, insightful, and a fair grader and still get bad evaluations because of how his/her unpleasant emotional state affects the classroom. Untreated depression and other mental health issues are huge obstacles to teaching. Attending to your sanity (which may include taking medication or making lifestyle changes) and practicing compassion (including self-compassion) will have a bigger impact on students than the best-written syllabus in the world."

FROM THE TRENCHES

Learn to Be a Performer

Carol Holstead, University of Kansas

Teaching in front of a class is an interactive performance that affects how closely students pay attention and what they will remember. Performance is a skill that does not come naturally to most people, and students are critics. They can't help it. When they see you in front of them several times a week, they will notice all your tics, your mannerisms, your tone of voice and your interaction with them (not to mention memorize your entire wardrobe)."

Like any other skill, the performance part of teaching is something you have to develop. Everyone has his or her own presentation style. You don't have to be an extrovert or a comedian to succeed, but you do have to master your voice, mannerisms and interaction with students.

- **Become self-aware.**
  Have a colleague watch you teach and tell you what you're doing. Do you pace back and forth? Do you use filler words like "um" and "you know" a lot? Do you stare at your notes or the screen and not the class? Are you spinning your arms like a windmill? Whatever you're doing, you will notice it more yourself once someone points it out to you. Then you have to make a conscious effort to change that behavior. Paying attention to your talking and physical presence and how the class is reacting becomes easier with experience. Eventually you'll be able to notice, while still talking, that you're only speaking to the left side of the room, that you keep pointing at the class, and that someone in the back row is looking at her phone.
- **Get out from behind the podium.**
  If there's space, walk and talk. I teach a class of 100 students in stadium seating, and I walk up and down the aisles while talking so I can look at individual students in the back of the room.
- **Animate.**
  Bring energy and enthusiasm for what you're teaching to class. If you tend to be low key, think about what you're saying, and be attentive, as you would be in a conversation.
- **Have a conversation.**
  Think of lecturing as chatting with individual students, not as talking to a class. This will help you to gesture and speak more naturally. In conversations we tend not to exhibit the same bad habits we have in front of an audience. (Except for filler words such as "like." People who say "like" a lot tend to say it in every speaking situation.)

FROM THE TRENCHES

Be Comfortable with Imperfection

Lani Diane Rich, Syracuse University

Being a good teacher is about connecting with your students, and you do that best by being as genuinely yourself as you can be. There's a tendency while teaching to want to be invulnerable, to be perfect, to be above reproach, and I think that can make it harder for us to see and correct the mistakes we make.

By incorporating vulnerability into my teaching, I take the pressure off myself to be perfect. If I make a mistake, I'm open about it. If I don't know an answer, I'll say I don't know but will find out and get back to the students. If I'm thinking out loud and not sure my off-the-cuff theorizing is quite right, I openly acknowledge that as well.

This gives me a level of comfort with imperfection, which allows me to self-correct without shame. It makes it easier for the students to give me feedback or jump into the conversation with critical thought. It also makes it easier for me to sort their feedback into the things that are really a problem and the things that the students are just complaining about. For instance, students' being uncomfortable with subject matter is not my problem. Some of the most important topics that need discussion are uncomfortable, and that's a good thing. However, if I discuss these topics in a way that is unintentionally offensive or unclear and confusing, I want to know so I can correct for that.

By cutting myself some slack on the perfection front, I make it easier to see clearly where I can do better and self-correct.

CLASSROOM OBSERVATION CHECKLIST

This checklist is designed to be a guide for the preparation of a narrative report that includes appropriate items on the list. Not all the items may be applicable in a given class, and observers are encouraged to add other comments.

The Situation
- Number and name of the course, and date and time of the observation
- What is the course enrollment and how many students were present?
- What is the primary teaching method? (lecture, lab, question and answer)
- Were there problems in the physical surroundings (lighting, acoustics, seating arrangements, audiovisual equipment, etc.) that might have affected teaching and learning in this room?

Structure and Goals
- Did the teacher's presentation show signs of planning and organization?
- Did the teacher integrate instructional elements (lecture, blackboard materials, handouts, audiovisual materials) effectively?
- Did the teacher use class time efficiently?
- Did the teacher respond appropriately to unanticipated situations?

Teaching Behaviors
- Did the teacher exhibit enthusiasm for teaching and for the subject?
- Was the teacher active enough? Too active?
- Did the teacher maintain appropriate eye contact with students?
- Did the teacher speak at a proper speed for comprehension and interest?
- Did the teacher use language and terminology that was understandable to students?
- Did the teacher ask and answer questions appropriately?
- How did the teacher's style contribute to learning?
- Did the teacher exhibit distracting mannerisms?

Subject Manner
- Was the depth and breadth of the material appropriate to the course and students?
- Did the teacher seem to have mastery of the material?
- Did the teacher incorporate recent developments and new knowledge?

Teacher-Student Rapport
- Did the teacher demonstrate fair and equitable concern for students?
- Did students seem receptive to the teacher's presentation?
- Were students generally receptive?
- Was the teacher accessible and receptive to students before and after class?

General
- What are the strong points about this teacher's classroom style and performance?
- What concrete suggestions can you offer to help the teacher do a better job?

Source: UNC-Chapel Hill School of Media and Journalism

9

Beyond the Classroom

Natalie T. J. Tindall, Lamar University

Unlike the other chapters in this book, this chapter has very little to do with classroom management practices. Instead, the focus is on the mechanisms that allow you to do the best job you can in the classroom: things such as securing an appropriate paycheck, developing a writing strategy that can build your case for tenure and inform your teaching and dealing with campus and departmental politics.

This chapter will offer micro-tips and tools that others and I have used to get through the tenure track to tenure. This chapter does not address the many macro issues that affect and hamper the route to tenure, such as the latent and blatant -isms that are embedded in the academy and the tenure process. They do exist and provide an obstacle course (Ragins and Sundstrom 1989) for those seeking tenure and promotion. Other scholars do a great job addressing these issues.

I am not ignoring the latent and active macro issues and various -isms that surround the tenure process or life in the academy (e.g., racism, sexism, heterosexism, audism, abilism). Other scholars have done and continue to do a great job documenting the structural conditions, effects and solutions within universities. These are just micro-tips and tools for those who are in tenure-track lines that I used and that others have used to get through the macro-hoops of tenure. Use and apply at your own benefit.

NEGOTIATING SALARY AND OTHER TERMS

Congratulations! You've made it through the obstacle course we call the interview process, and you have arrived on the other side, triumphant, somewhat battered and the declared winner of the jobs race. You are the candidate that the department wants to hire. After the jubilation dies down, you then realize that you have to start the negotiation process. You realize that negotiating is necessary in order for you to be compensated fairly, but how do you do it? Where do you go from here?

Read up on the process. The basics of negotiation are the same for all jobs. It is in your best interest to review blogs and delve into books that discuss the topic. Start with Karen Kelsy's blog and her book "The Professor Is In" as well as Wendy Crone's "Survive and Thrive: A Guide for Untenured Faculty." Other nonacademic books for negotiation include Roger Fisher, William Ury and Bruce Patton's "Getting to Yes" (1992) and Roger Fisher and Scott Brown's "Getting Together" (1989).

Understand who you are talking to. During your interview, you should have met the person with whom you will negotiate. You should understand that person's on-campus role and their role in the hiring process, and from the interview you should have gleaned what their concerns are for the role. The micro-needs of a department chair (having someone to cover specific, detailed content area, building a congenial culture) might be polarizingly different from the macro- and meso-wants of the provost or dean such as moving the college into a higher ranking, building a research culture, or moving the university into commercial research interests. In all negotiations, you have to know the other party and what the other party wants. The best offense is a good defense, so prepare yourself by knowing the perspective of the hiring manager who has to negotiate with shrinking financial conditions, increasing university demands, union contracts and other policies in mind.

Ask questions. If you didn't talk in depth with the hiring manager, now is the time to start. Talk with the hiring manager and ask questions that will "clarify his/her desires, priorities, and needs" (Adjunct Professor Link n.d.). Doing this will give you the opportunity to develop win-win solutions that achieve the hiring manager's interests and your best interests.

Know your deal-breakers. All jobs are not created equal, and all salary negotiations are not explicit. As a candidate, you need to have a firm understanding of what matters to you and your career. Think through what items you must have and would like for your new job. Some considerations beyond salary (which is priority No. 1) might include:

1. Start-up funding;
2. Moving expenses;
3. Conference travel;
4. Teaching releases;

5. Paid visit to look for housing;
6. Summer salary;
7. Credit toward tenure (if you have worked on the tenure track elsewhere);
8. Teaching load;
9. Spousal hire (Crone 2010; Kelsky 2014).

Estimate your costs. Now that you know what you must have, build an estimate for your hiring package.

Pick a number, not just any number. According to Matti Keloharju, you shouldn't use round numbers for your salary and negotiation package. "If you do not have any more precise information on the value of . . . your labor than your negotiating partner, there is little point in advertising your lack of information by posting a round offer," said Keloharju. From the research, this strategy results in getting the amount desired—with interest.

Get everything in writing. Documentation is key. Reply to emails with lists or bullets detailing the finer points of the negotiation. Building a paper trail will only help you for the future. For example, a faculty member and a dean may have had a verbal agreement about course load, computer software and hardware and start-up funding, but when the dean retires or moves, there is no record of that agreement. Do not get burned. Keep a record to confirm and keep the negotiation transparent to all parties.

Consider your sources and take stock of your resources. Everyone in your home academic department and in your life will have advice about what you should and should not do with this job offer. All advice is not equal, and all advice is not good. Before rushing to seek out advice or soaking in well-intentioned words of wisdom, take a step back and consider whether the faculty members giving advice are knowledgeable about the current shape of the marketplace.

Follow the money. Research the salaries for the department, the college, and the university. This is easier for public institutions; however, a generic snapshot of the data for private schools may be available. In a column for Inside Higher Education, Adam Fulton (2011) recommended this strategy because "it will give you the most realistic information of how high the dean will be able to go. Additionally, you should seek out similar data from peer institutions located in the same geographic area. This information might give you leverage to push the dean higher by making a case that the institution is out of sync with its peer institutions. I would suggest that your request not go beyond about 6 percent of the original offer."

For contingent faculty, negotiation may be limited or does not exist. If you can negotiate, do. Some additional considerations for you may include:

- If you are asked to teach a new course, is there a course development fee "to compensate [you] for time spent working on it before the semester starts"? (Thaler 2015)
- Is the class capped at a certain number? If the class exceeds the cap, do you receive additional monies for the course?

FINDING TIME FOR YOUR OWN RESEARCH AND WRITING

Now that you are on campus in your new job, new demands will present themselves in many ways. As professors, we are expected to sandwich research, writing, grading, teaching, administering, mentoring, advising and service appointments into our work weeks. The discernible percentages we are told about—40 percent teaching, 20 percent service and 40 percent research—can become lopsided at various points in the semester. (Personally, every spring when I did not have administrative duties, I felt that it is 82.5 percent service, 82.5 percent teaching, and 0 percent research. Nothing added up to the amounts I was told and held accountable for.) Our lives as professors are a series of clashing obligations, and, during certain points, our lives feel like they belong to someone else. Faced with the demands of students and the press of administrative minutiae (travel forms, hello!), our research may pull the short straw during the year.

Here are some strategies for putting your research back into rotation:

Acknowledge that you are a professional writer. As academics, we write syllabi, proposals, papers, book chapters and textbooks. Even with all that writing, we forget or don't consider that we are professional writers. This means we must work continually to improve our craft. Improvement comes with practice, so start writing. Do what you need and want to do when it comes to your writing.

Protect your time. Time is "crucial for the structuring and direction of everyday lives. Time can furthermore be used as an instrument of power and control" (Davies 1989, 17). If you don't protect your time, no one else will. Be honest and use the word "no" often to avoid taking on additional responsibilities and roles. There are periods of time that you cannot control. For those times you can, you should make space for the activities that are vital to your career and self-care. Schedule your writing and your research. Understand what works best for you, examine your writing practices and block your schedule accordingly. For some professors with caregiving responsibilities, they write when their children are napping or at daycare. For some nocturnal professors, they opt to write in the late night or early morning hours because that is when they are intellectually sharp.

Spend time developing your writing voice. This means that you must work on improving your writing. Read writers you admire. Read about the craft of writing. Write for fun. Write for work and the places you frequent out of work (your friend's business, your house of worship, your community group, your neighborhood association). But you need to write and practice often.

Join a writing group and join a writing accountability group. Start a faculty writers group with colleagues in your department or across the university. A writing group may take various forms, but at the most basic level, you bring your writing to the group for comment and critique or you write with the group for a set period of time. At Lamar University, during the summer, we have Writing Wednesdays, where the sixth floor of the library is open for faculty to fire up a laptop and write. (For resources on how to set up such a group, visit the University of North Carolina's Writing Center's Writing Group Startup Kit.) I would also advise that you belong to or start up or join an accountability group. I use the agraphia group concept from Paul Silvia's (2007) "How to Write A Lot," which he described as "a structured writing group focused on concrete writing goals. In a typical agraphia group, the members meet and set specific goals for what they'll write before the next meeting. The group's record-keeper writes the goals down for posterity, and the next week's meeting starts with checking off which goals were met and unmet" (Silvia 2011).

Rely on your selected academic and personal community. Community can be found online or in person. Have a support network of helpful colleagues, friends, family and acquaintances that will allow you to air grievances as well as celebrate when the dossier is submitted. Vent to your colleagues, and use them as a sounding board and mastermind group. Use your community to get out of the house, your office and your thoughts. Join friends for dinner, go camping, try a new dance class or develop a new knitting pattern.

Find research and writing mentors in your field and at your university. Mentoring is a relationship between two people that will change over time. Sometimes it is formalized by organizations or associations. Sometimes it is an organic relationship that emerges out of a talk over coffee or bonding at a retreat. Find people who are in the same area as you, and ask them for help and guidance with writing and publishing. Ask your mentors to review your research agenda and dossier. Tap your mentors for insight that you cannot readily obtain from colleagues. If you don't know where to find a mentor, look at the professors who have careers you admire and ask them. Many people are flattered when they are asked to serve as a mentor.

Natalie T. J. Tindall

Avoid certain people. At the same time as you develop mentors and find a community, you should avoid certain people who cause your anxiety or blood pressure to spike. You can't become a hermit, but refrain from engaging in conversations about the path to promotion and tenure with certain people. If you must entertain them, keep the conversations to a minimum. You cannot afford to let the doubts, frustrations and maladies of others take up space in your head as you confront this process. Ask questions to those with wise counsel and few tenure horror stories.

Read your promotion and tenure manual early and often. There is the temptation to avoid looking at the manual until the point when you must know how to compile your physical and electronic tenure dossier. Don't do that. To know your department, college and university's expectations, read all the manuals early in your career and prepare accordingly. Don't analyze to the point of paralysis. Ask your dean, director and/or chair for clarity about their expectations and the guidelines set forth by the university and the college. Do not rely upon your own understanding.

Develop a clear plan for your writing across multiple semesters. Always have a plan. My parents taught me that early, and I had never applied this to my career until I started my first tenure-track job. At the start of your career, create at minimum a three-semester agenda with the goal being tenure. Plan and have smart goals with concrete strategies. Take a sheet of paper and have three columns, one for service, teaching and research.

For each year, think about the big bricks of your career path:

- What goals do you want to achieve?
- What outcomes do you desire to have?
- What are the things you need to do per your research, your P&T manual, your department's expectations?
- What research do you need to finish? What is in your research pipeline? What projects do you want to start?
- What teaching innovations do you want to integrate into your classroom?
- What are the things you want to do for your own career development, personal development, and teaching development?

(For an example, you can view an older version of such a plan via this link: http://bit.ly/2tGDZts.)

This is your chance to shape your research trajectory and agenda (which we talk about often in many graduate programs yet never fully build out), but also gives you a method to shape your teaching and service goals and to determine how those goals can meet and intersect with your writing and publishing demands. Reflect on this before and after you complete it. As you get things done on your lists, mark them off. As you change and grow in your career, some items may not be needed any more so delete or change. But at least create a plan (on your terms) for your own trajectory.

FROM THE TRENCHES

Chris Roush, UNC-Chapel Hill

I became a full-time, tenure-track professor in 2002 after spending the previous three years as an adjunct or visiting professor at three separate universities. Suddenly, I was thrust into a world where my future depended on publishing articles and building an agenda focused around my area of interest. In addition to teaching three classes a semester, that was not easy.

I started slowly. My first semester, I published an op-ed in the local newspaper, and luckily my university accepted it as something that could be counted when I went up for tenure. I also started looking around at what was needed in my field, which happens to be business journalism.

That's how I came up with the idea of writing a business journalism textbook. The ones that I was using to teach were sorely out of date and didn't cover some of the concepts that I was teaching in my class. So I asked some faculty colleagues for contacts at academic publishers, and soon I had a contract. The book practically wrote itself because it was material that I had already put together to teach my classes. The publication of that book helped me get tenure.

I've gone on to write other books and refereed journal articles as well as magazine articles and more newspaper op-eds. They've all been about things that I was personally interested in, and they all were tangentially related to business journalism.

I've always used fear of failure as a big motivator to push myself to find the time to write, and with tenure looming over my head, that helped. But I'd also encourage anyone to find a research or writing agenda that is focused and specific. You'd be amazed at the different ways you can find to write about your interest, and that helps you maintain your academic standing and build your reputation.

DEPARTMENT AND CAMPUS POLITICS

Academic politics is the most vicious and bitter form of politics, because the stakes are so low.

—Wallace Stanley Sayre (1905–1972), U.S. political
scientist and professor at Columbia University

Department and campus politics vary at every institution. Someone will not like someone else. Some researcher will believe that his or her approach and methodology is superior to her colleagues'. Some contingent of the faculty will believe that their area needs more resources, more money and more pretty and shiny things than another area. Some faculty members will use alternative facts and exaggerations to distort their records. Some faculty are just horrible people and will be either ostracized or elevated in a department. Even the most Lake Woebegone–type campus will have department and campus politics. The politics and the personalities were there before you were hired, and they will be there after you leave.

In academia, there are two categories of faculty: "I'm here to make friends" camp and the "I'm not here to make friends—I'm here to win" camp. In the "I'm here to make friends" camp, you keep your eyes on the prize: tenure, research or creative activity, and stay out of the fray. You play nice with everyone and try to collaborate with everyone. The "I'm not here to make friends" camp views everything as a competition. It's you versus everyone else, and you align yourself with the group that can give you the quickest route and access to power and resources. Any avid watcher of reality television will know that the people in the former camp never win. In academia, where the rules of life are occasionally subverted, people with this belief do win, but not always.

BALANCING WORK AND LIFE

Work-life balance is a media-created myth. Even researchers have abandoned the term (for the most part). However, the "inter-role conflict in which the role pressures from the work and family domains are mutually incompatible in some respect" (M. Hogan and V. Hogan 2007) has been the prime research area for this topic, and rightly so. According to Jeffrey Greenhaus and Nicholas Beutell (1985), the strains that prompt this conflict come from three places:

- Time conflict: "Time spent on activities within one role generally cannot be devoted to activities within another role." (p. 79)
- Role-produced strain, which is defined as happening when "one role affects one's performance in another role. The roles are incompatible in the sense that the strain created by one makes it difficult to comply with the demands of another." (p. 80)
- Behavior-based strain, when the role you have and the elements of your life have distinct and incompatible behavioral norms and value systems.

Acknowledge the "greediness" of the career you have opted into and the institution where you work. Lewis Coser (1974) wrote that the greedy organizations ask for complete "undivided and exclusive" loyalty and that the institution's "demands on the person are omnivorous" (p. 4). In her discussion of contemporary greedy organizations, Marianne Egger de Campo claimed that these greedy organizations "demand undivided time and loyalty from the individual who will voluntarily devote him/herself for exclusive benefits only granted to loyal followers" (2013, 969). This is done through creating an "aura of exclusivity" (Burchielli, Bartram and Thanacoody 2008) and by pressuring individual members to "weaken their ties, or not form any ties, with other institutions or persons that might make claims that conflict with their own [organizational] demands" (Coser 1974, 6).

Let's face it: Modern employers, including your campus institution and its web of social actors (students, department chairs, committees, etc.), are greedy for your time, attention and energy. They are the bureaucratic version of the Audrey II (the flower from the movie "Little Shop of Horrors"), always asking for you to feed them. However, personal strategies can help you reduce the anxiety and conflict between roles and harness the greediness of your institution.

Look for colleges, universities and organizations with explicit structural work-life support. Work-life integration requires both structural work-life support and cultural work-life support. The latter happens at the organizational level where job structures and human resources allow workers the flexibility to control his or her work activities and provide "additional instrumental resources such as information and direct services to enable individuals to be able to combine employment with caregiving or other important non-work roles" (Kossek, Lewis and Hammer 2010).

Some examples of structural support are:

- teleworking and virtual arrangements;
- reduced workloads;
- formal policies on absenteeism, vacations, and sick time that support work–life needs;
- enhanced childcare and eldercare benefits (vouchers, care assistance).

Not only should there be structures in place, but there should be open communication about the universal policies and procedures for using those structures as well as supervisory emotional and instrumental support. Since supervisors "are the gatekeepers to effective implementation of work and family policies" (Ryan and Kosseck 2008), it is important for faculty that their department chairs, college deans and other immediate supervisors are supportive and work toward implementing the universal policies.

Develop your agency. Creating a life where you can juggle and integrate the demands and joys of both a career and a life relies upon agency. Natalie Tindall and Markesha McWilliams (2011) define agency as the self-created, self-orchestrated and intentional method of garnering the "power, will, and desire to create work contexts conducive to the development of their thought over time" (Neumann, Terosky and Schell 2006, 92-93).

Academics exist at the intersection of privileged existence and forced impositions. We have the privilege and ability to shape our lives and choices, yet we often fall into the expectations of what and who an academic should be, get trapped into believing that the guidelines of the tenure and promotion document define us. The identity of being a professor can become the singular role we play and have in our lives.

In hoity-toity academic terms, agency is "the capacity of an agent (a person or other entity) to act in a world." In the plain-speak terminology that is required outside the ivory tower, agency is your efficacy to do you. Put even more simply, I had to ask the question: What the hell is stopping me from doing what I want, going after what I want, and getting what I need?"

REFERENCES

Adjunct Professor Link. (n.d.) "Negotiating Your Contract: Do's and Don'ts." https://adjunctprofessorlink.com/blog/best-practices-for-teaching/Negotiating-Your-Contract--Do-s-and-Don-ts.

Burchielli, R., T. Bartram and R. Thanacoody (2008). "Work-Family Balance Or Greedy Organizations?" Relations Industrielles/Industrial Relations 108-133.

Coser, L. A. (1974). Greedy Institutions: Patterns of Undivided Commitment. New York: The Free Press.

Crone, W. C. (2010). Survive and Thrive: A Guide for Untenured Faculty. University of Wisconsin-Madison. Williston, VT: Morgan and Claypool.

Davies, K. (1989). Women and Time: Weaving the Strands of Everyday Life. Lund: Grahns Boktryckeri.

Egger de Campo, M. (2013). "Contemporary Greedy Institutions: An Essay on Lewis Coser's Concept in the Era of the 'Hive Mind.'" Sociologický časopis/Czech Sociological Review 969-987.

Fisher, R., and S. Brown (1989). Getting Together: Building Relationships as We Negotiate. New York: Penguin.

Fisher, R., W. Ury and B. Patton (1992). Getting to Yes: Negotiating Agreement Without Giving In. 2nd ed. New York: Houghton Mifflin Harcourt.

Fulton, A. (March 14, 2011). "Negotiate Like a Professor." https://www.inside highered.com/advice/2011/03/14/essay_on_how_to_negotiate_during_the_ academic_job_process.

Greenhaus, J. H., and N. J. Beutell (1985). "Sources of Conflict Between Work and Family Roles." Academy of Management Review 10 (1): 76-88.

Gregory, A., and S. Milner (2009). "Editorial: Work-Life Balance: A Matter of Choice?" Gender, Work and Organization 16 (1): 1-13.

Hogan, M., and V. Hogan (2007). "Work-Life Integration." The Irish Psychologist 22 (10): 246-254.

Keloharju, M. (March 15, 2016). "Don't Use Round Numbers in a Negotiation." https://hbr.org/2016/03/dont-use-round-numbers-in-a-negotiation.

Kelsky, K. (March 24, 2014). "OK, Let's Talk About Negotiating Salary." https:// chroniclevitae.com/news/400-the-professor-is-in-ok-let-s-talk-about-negotiat ing-salary.

———. (2015). The Professor Is In: The Essential Guide to Turning Your PhD into a Job. New York: Three Rivers Press.

Kossek, E., S. Lewis and L. B. Hammer (2010). "Work-Life Initiatives and Organizational Change: Overcoming Mixed Messages to Move from the Margin to the Mainstream." Human Relations 63 (1): 3-19.

Neumann, A., Terosky, A. L., and Schell, J. (2006). Agents of learning: Strategies for assuming agency, for learning, in tenured faculty careers. In S. J. Bracken, J. K. Allen and D. R. Dean (Eds.), The Balancing Act: Gendered Perspectives in Faculty Roles and Work Lives. Sterling, VA: Stylus Publishing.

Ragins, B. R., and E. Sundstrom (1989). "Gender and Power in Organizations: A Longitudinal Perspective." Psychological Bulletin 105 (1): 51-88.

Robbins, S. P. (2016). "Finding Your Voice as an Academic Writer (and Writing Clearly)." Journal of Social Work Education 52 (2): 133-135.

Ryan, A. M., and E. E. Kossek (2008). "Work–Life Policy Implementation: Breaking Down or Creating Barriers to Inclusiveness?" Human Resource Management 47 (2): 295-310.

Silvia, P. J. (2007). How to Write A Lot: A Practical Guide to Productive Academic Writing. Washington, DC: American Psychological Association.

———. (2011). "Procrastination: On Writing Tomorrow What You Should Have Written Last Year." http://blog.apastyle.org/apastyle/2011/05/procrastina tion-on-writing-tomorrow-what-you-should-have-written-last-year.html.

Thaler, A. (May 20, 2015). Negotiating Your Way to a Fair Adjuncting Experience. https://chroniclevitae.com/news/997-negotiating-your-way-to-a-fair-adjunct ing-experience.

Tindall, N. J. J., and McWilliams, M. S. (2011). The myth and mismatch of balance: Black female professors' construction of balance, integration, and negotiation of work and life. In E. Gilchrist (Ed.)., Experiences of Single African-American Female Professors: With This Ph.D, I thee Wed. Lanham, MD: Lexington.

Index

About the Contributors

Catherine Cassara is an associate professor at Bowling Green State University, where she teaches journalism history, international press and public affairs reporting. She has taught at the graduate and undergraduate level. Before entering academia, Cassara worked at newspapers in Connecticut and Maine. Cassara has been head of the journalism department of Bowling Green since 2002.

William G. Christ is a professor at Trinity University in San Antonio. In 1999, he was named the International Radio and Television Society Foundation's Stephen H. Coltrin Professor of the Year. In 2012, he received the Broadcast Education Association Distinguished Education Service Award. He has been writing about issues in media education for over 40 years, concentrating on curriculum and assessment. He holds a master's degree from the University of Wisconsin and a PhD from Florida State University.

Charles N. Davis is the dean of the Henry W. Grady College of Journalism and Mass Communication at the University of Georgia. He spent 14 years as a professor at the University of Missouri School of Journalism. His teaching awards include the Scripps Howard Foundation National Journalism Teacher of the Year Award in 2008, the Provost's Award for Junior Faculty Teaching in 2001 and the University of Missouri Alumni Association's Faculty/Alumni Award in 2008.

Jennifer Jacobs Henderson is a professor and chair of the Department of Communication at Trinity University in San Antonio, Texas. Her research addresses issues of media law, the ethics of media and the use of participatory cultures for political and social action. Aligned with her work as department chair, she has also recently been publishing about media education and assessment.

Susan Keith is an associate professor and chair of the Department of Journalism and Media Studies in the School of Communication and Information at Rutgers University. At Rutgers, she teaches face-to-face, online-only, and hybrid courses in media law and policy on the undergraduate, master's and PhD levels and courses in media ethics, editing and design, and international journalism to undergraduates. Her research focuses on the content of media, especially visual media; coverage of war and conflict; media ethics and law; and the transformation of journalists' work. She was as a journalist for 16 years before earning a PhD from the University of North Carolina at Chapel Hill. She lives in New York City with her husband and daughter.

Earnest L. Perry is an associate professor at the University of Missouri School of Journalism. Perry's research interests focus on African-American press history and media management. He received a second-place award from the Association for Education in Journalism and Mass Communication in 2002 for his paper on the African-American press's negotiation for a White House correspondent. Perry worked as a reporter for newspapers in Illinois, Connecticut and Texas before joining the school. He has also served as a consultant to news outlets in Texas and Missouri on issues such as newsroom management, reporting in ethnic minority communities, news writing and editing.

Mary T. Rogus is an associate professor at Ohio University. Her primary teaching responsibilities include "TV News Producing," "Broadcast News Seminar" and the "Newscast Practicum" class. She also teaches "Radio News," "TV News Reporting," "Advanced Public Affairs Reporting" and "Media Ethics," and developed a course in "TV News Election Coverage." Rogus received Ohio University's highest teaching honor, being named a Presidential Teacher for 2006-2009.

Chris Roush is the Walter E. Hussman Sr. Distinguished Professor in Business Journalism at University of North Carolina-Chapel Hill. In 2010, he was named Journalism Teacher of the Year by the Scripps Howard Foundation and the Association for Education in Journalism and Mass Communication. The judges noted that Roush "has become the expert in business journalism—not just at Chapel Hill, but throughout the country and even in other parts of the world." He has also been named the

North Carolina Professor of the Year by the Carnegie Foundation for the Advancement of Teaching and Council for Advancement and Support of Education.

Carol B. Schwalbe is an associate professor and director of graduate studies at the University of Arizona School of Journalism. Her research focuses on the role of images in shaping ideas and public opinion during the early years of the Cold War, ethical concerns about publishing violent images and the visual framing of the Iraq War on the internet. She teaches classes on editing and in 2011 launched a science journalism curriculum for the School of Journalism.

Natalie T. J. Tindall is an associate professor and director at Lamar University. Tindall has undertaken research in areas including identity, diversity and power in the public relations function; identity and health messages; fundraising and philanthropy; organizational culture and stereotypes within historically black fraternities and sororities; and the intersection of public relations and marketing with minority health. Her research has been published in the Public Relations Review, Howard Journal of Communications, PRism, and the Journal of Public Relations Research, with a considerable number of other projects moving through the publication process.

Leslie-Jean Thornton is an associate professor at Arizona State University. She previously taught editing and design, feature writing, reporting, newspaper management and "U.S. Press History and Internet Effects"—a course she proposed and created—at the State University of New York at New Paltz; editing, writing and reporting at Mercy College (New York) and editing and design at Old Dominion University (Virginia). She taught in the Dow Jones Newspaper Fund editing internship program in summer 2005.

Karen M. Turner is an associate professor at Temple University, where she teaches radio news reporting, the TUTV interview program "A Broader View" and since 1997 the online course "Race and Racism in the News." She was selected to attend the 2014 Temple Provost Teaching Academy and is a 2013 Lindback Foundation Distinguished Teaching awardee. She was the inaugural recipient (2004) of the School of Communications and Theater's Innovative Teaching award. Her research interests include diversity issues in media and the integration of new media technologies in race studies and journalism pedagogy. While working as a city hall reporter for Philadelphia's WPEN-AM, she worked side by side with WRTI-FM (Temple University Public Radio) student reporters, which motivated her to become a professor.